INNER LANDSCAPES

RON MOTTRAM

INNER LANDSCAPES

THE THEATER OF SAM SHEPARD

A LITERARY FRONTIERS EDITION

UNIVERSITY OF MISSOURI PRESS

COLUMBIA, 1984

FOR   MY   FAMILY

Library of Congress Cataloging in Publication Data

Mottram, Ron.
  Inner Landscapes.

  (A Literary frontiers edition)
  Includes index.
  1. Shepard, Sam, 1943–   . 2. Dramatists, American—
20th century—Biography.   I. Title.   II. Series.
PS3569.H394Z77   1984   812′.54   84–50795
ISBN 0–8262–0452–X

CONTENTS

Introduction

Sam Shepard has so often been called the most important playwright of his generation that the statement goes almost unchallenged today. Especially curious, therefore, was Walter Kerr's review of Shepard's most recent play, *Fool for Love*. Kerr denounced not only the play but also the playwright, causing Clive Barnes, in a spirited defense of Shepard, to speculate on the reasons for this "most strange attack."

Although praise is the rule in contemporary Shepard criticism, Kerr's remarks—among other things he accused Shepard of being a cult dramatist—indicate a common confusion about Shepard's work. Even the critics who admire him readily confess, as did Frank Rich in the *New York Times*, that they find his work to be "fragmented and at times beyond exegesis." The real difficulty, however, is not that Shepard's plays especially resist analysis and interpretation but that the critics lack familiarity with the whole body of Shepard's work and the overall development of his career. Herein lies the paradox of Sam Shepard. He is, simultaneously, both talked about and little known, widely produced and poorly understood. A recent anthology of critical commentary, *American Dreams: The Imagination of Sam Shepard*, though useful, points up the disparate nature of what has been said about him and underscores the need for a more complete and unified treatment of his writing. My purpose is to respond to that need by providing a critical overview of Shepard's career that, though far from exhaustive, offers a chronology of his accomplishments and an interpretative reading of his plays, which will, I hope, make a positive contribution to the ongoing dialogue about this extraordinary writer.

While I have concerned myself primarily with Shepard's plays, I have found it useful to relate them to his two collections of nondramatic writing, *Hawk Moon* and *Motel Chronicles*, as well as to the few brief essays on theater that he has published. His film career, however, both as an actor and screenwriter, I mention only in passing, leaving a fuller treatment to some other time. Finally, I have incorporated relevant biographical material in the form of both objective fact and Shepard's own imaginative recreation of his life in the characters and incidents of his plays.

The book is divided into five parts: Chapter One concerns Shepard's early life, the influence of his family, his move to New York at age nineteen, and the writing and production of his first two plays, *Cowboys* and *The Rock Garden*; Chapter Two considers the plays of the sixties and Shepard's rise from relative obscurity in the Off Off Broadway theater to a position of importance as one of America's most prominent young playwrights; Chapter Three looks at the crisis that developed in Shepard's life and work in the early seventies, his move to England in 1971, the growing influence of music on his plays, his return to America in 1974, and the transitional plays of the mid-seventies; Chapter Four examines Shepard's career since 1976, a period marked by the "family trilogy"—*Curse of the Starving Class*, the Pulitzer Prize–winning *Buried Child*, and *True West*—and culminating in his recent production, *Fool for Love*; and, finally, Chapter Five summarizes Shepard's career and raises the question of his future development.

The plays of Sam Shepard are rich in culturally and theatrically coded signs. They are literally constructed from elements that have an established semantic dimension: characters based on specific models in myth, history, and contemporary reality; music made famous by important rock bands; settings and actions that play heavily on the iconography of Hollywood, rural America, middle-class suburbia, the nineteenth-century West, and the automobile. This intensive accumulation of signs from both reality and other artistic media constitutes more than a field of reference: it is at the heart of the very language by which Shepard expresses meaning and communicates his vision of America. This language of images, actions, setting, cultural icons, and character types is, of course, made up of natural language combined, by means of staging technique, with a language of movement and gesture. The commonly held critical notion that Shepard appeals essentially to the senses rather than to the mind is fundamentally a denial of Shepard's cultural framework, and consequently a denial of what is of the greatest significance in Shepard's work, his perceptions about America and what it means to be alive in America in the second half of the twentieth century.

In his method of representation Shepard resembles two writers for whom he has expressed admiration, Samuel Beckett and Bertolt Brecht, though he has rejected the philosophical abstraction of one and the ideological absoluteness of the other in favor of a flexible social criticism that explores the simultaneous alienation and integration of the individual in American society. The model for this individual is Sam Shepard himself, an artist who, like his mentors of the beat generation, rejects the corrupt and corrupting values of the society and insists on exposing its violent contradictions, but only because he is profoundly of that society and sees its current manifestations as part of his own inner landscape. As a result, Sam Shepard sings not only of America but also of himself.

I. On the Road: "From Some Place to Some Place"

The first place was cold, a "freezing morning." The first morning. The windows of the hospital room looked out over Lake Michigan, and his mother, worn out from the ordeal of birth, did not see her newborn son drag his body across the floor toward the windows, nor was she aware of his attempts to pull himself up to where he could see the world outside. The room was suffused with a pale green light that reflected off the green icebergs that already choked the lake, even though it was still early November. A humming sound, which turned into the drone of war-planes, brought panic to the child. He found himself free from one world, the world of her body, but unable to move adequately in his new world. He was having his first lesson in suffering and did not know where to turn.[1]

Another version of Sam Shepard's birth records that he changed worlds on 5 November 1943 at Fort Sheridan, Illinois, an army base not far from Chicago. His father, Samuel Shepard Rogers, was serving as a bomber pilot in Europe at the time, leaving his mother, Jane Schook Rogers, to cope with the newborn child herself.

Still another version places Shepard's birth in the Hopi Hawk Moon month, "month of cold set in" and secret whispers on the high mesa, of "signs of barren empty need for prayer," accompanied by sounds of the ancient Snake and Antelope ceremony and the shocking image of men and boys dancing with live rattlesnakes in their mouths to prove their manliness and fearlessness and to bring on much-needed rain.[2]

All three versions are true, as long as one does not mea-

1. Sam Shepard, *Motel Chronicles* (San Francisco: City Lights Books, 1982), pp. 52–53.
2. *Hawk Moon* (New York: Performing Arts Journal Publications, 1973), p. 11.

sure truth by simple, prosaic facts alone but is willing to listen to the imaginative renderings of the artist as he re-creates his own life. More than any objective accounting, the biographic testimony found in Sam Shepard's writing gives access to an inner landscape that deepens our under-standing of both the man and his work. This testimony is found throughout his plays and is particularly prominent in his most recent collection of published prose, *Motel Chronicles*.

That Sam Shepard relates his birth in one account to an act of separation ("I knew I was away from her body now. Separate.") and in another to a ritual of integration (through the Snake ceremony Hopi boys gained member-ship in a fraternity of men) is significant. Both, of course, are rites of passage requiring physical exertion, a move-ment toward a goal. In each of the accounts, however, the goal is different, and this difference characterizes one of the problems of contemporary American culture that She-pard explores in his plays. The conclusion of the infant's struggle, initiated, as Shepard describes it, by a sudden plunge into the world, is a suspended state: "I watched her body. I knew I'd come from her body but I wasn't sure how. . . . I felt a tremendous panic suddenly. I was be-tween these two worlds. The world I'd left behind and this new one. I had no idea where to turn." For the Hopi youth, however, the successful participation in the Snake cere-mony, though a fearful ordeal, results in a state of comple-tion, of membership in a stable and satisfying community that fully defines the role and place of the individual. As the products of a fragmented society, one that at best has lost its sense of community, we, along with Sam Shepard, can never achieve such a sense of wholeness. We are, among other things, a society without significant and uni-fying rituals. In sharp contrast, the image of the Hopi runs through much of Shepard's writing and suggests to us at least what we are lacking as a culture and, therefore, where some of our ills lie.

Ultimately, the Hopi ritual is a spiritual journey that gives significant meaning to human activity, but without the ultimate spiritual meaning the human activity becomes problematic. The energy, the need to plunge into the world and reach the windows that are the threshold of experience, continues to exist. It gives rise to movement, even if the movement leads to no particular place; when the place is not the goal, the movement itself takes on primary significance.

Fort Sheridan, then, was just another place, even though for Sam Shepard it was the first place. When his father returned home wounded, a piece of shrapnel permanently embedded in the back of his neck, the family began a series of moves that took them from army base to army base and that eventually landed them on Guam. Shepard recreates one of the early moves in *Motel Chronicles*.

Once again it is cold. The family Plymouth is crossing the Badlands at night, leaving Rapid City, *South* North Dakota, in the past. Sam is teething, and his mother has given him "ice cubes wrapped in napkins to suck on." They stop on the prairie to look at a collection of huge plaster dinosaurs, his mother carrying him around in an army blanket and humming "Peg a' My Heart."[3] The action is slight, but it is more significant than the place from which they have come, which Shepard does not even bother to describe; nor does he describe the place to which they are going.

The Badlands. For the early settlers of the West they were a place to get through, dangerous even for the creatures born there. For those out of their element, they could be deadly. In a short piece called "Deserted," which appears in the collection *Hawk Moon*, Shepard describes a pet snake let loose in the desert, an environment once natural for this creature but now become alien. Like the infant crawling away from its mother immediately after birth, the snake does not know where to go. It remains motionless: "frozen with vastness and uncertainty. The silent boom of desert. Deserted. Left to be wild and not knowing how anymore."[4] Despite its forbidding nature, however, the desert, as both a place and a passage, fascinates Shepard. It recurs repeatedly in his plays as a setting for the action and

3. *Motel Chronicles*, p. 9.
4. *Hawk Moon*, p. 31.

as a refuge for the absent father no longer able to live with his family, who at the extreme is alienated from all normal social contact. Rock singer Patti Smith, with whom Shepard lived for a short period, has summarized this fascination in an image of Shepard sitting in his Hudson Hornet, parked by the New York docks, the Badlands "pulsing through his anatomy."[5]

On that cold night among the dinosaurs, however, the pulsing longings that Patti Smith described were still a long way off. There were many other roads to travel and other places to link them. One place that Shepard has returned to a number of times in his writing is Guam, the image of which is dominated by several elements: rain, driving in a jeep (cars of one kind or another are a constant in Shepard's work), his mother shooting at Japanese soldiers who occasionally came out of the jungle to steal laundry off the clotheslines, and going to a drive-in movie to see Walt Disney's *Song of the South*. Shepard also describes himself sitting on the floor of the jeep wearing a cowboy hat and trying to shield his ears from the gunfire. The objective truth of this image cannot be established, but its significance as part of the legend of Sam Shepard cannot be denied. Traveling, the idea of the mother as guardian figure in the absence of the father, the cowboy and movie references—all are significant motifs in Shepard's career.

In the mid-fifties, Samuel Shepard Rogers, now out of the army, took his family to California, living for a time in Pasadena and finally settling in Duarte, where he began growing avocados and raising sheep. Sam Jr., known as Steve to his family and friends, helped on the ranch, attended school, went to the movies, tried to impress girls, began to grow alienated from his family, and dreamed of escaping.

Probably the ordinariness of things contributed to his desire to escape, the day-to-dayness of school, family, and chores. In *Motel Chronicles* Shepard describes a series of sleepwalking incidents that occurred during this time in

5. Patti Smith, "Sam Shepard: 9 Random Years [7 + 2]," in Sam Shepard, *Angel City, Curse of the Starving Class & Other Plays* (New York: Urizen Books, 1980), p. 245.

Duarte. Each time, his parents led him back to bed and in the morning told him what had happened. He imagined these nightly walks, which he could not remember, and looked forward to his parents' descriptions of them. So compelling did those "unconscious encounters" with his parents become that he decided to fake a sleepwalking incident in order to experience his parents' reactions firsthand. His parents caught him at this charade and told him that they did not find his escapade at all funny. "Humor," Shepard wrote, "was the furthest thing from my mind. It was only for the thrill of having a relationship with them outside the ordinary. A different kind of encounter."[6] The inability to achieve a different kind of encounter between parents and children underlies many of the domestic relationships that later formed an important part of his literary output.

As Shepard moved into his teenage years, there must have developed a widening gap between his imagination and the actuality of his life. Fed by movies, his imagination could take control. He remembers trying to imitate the smile of Burt Lancaster after seeing the film *Vera Cruz*. He practiced the smile in the backyard, exposing his front teeth in that grin for which Lancaster has become so famous. Then, he tried it on the girls at school, only to discover that they looked at him strangely, perhaps even with fear in their eyes. Under the spell of the Lancaster illusion, he had forgotten how bad his teeth were, how one was brown and another broken, hardly perfect like Lancaster's. Soon he stopped grinning and returned to his "empty face."[7] This hold of the movies on his imagination and desire has never left him. On 28 April 1981 he wrote, "I keep praying for a double bill of *Bad Day at Black Rock* and *Vera Cruz*," a prayer that could easily be shared by many moviegoers who came to consciousness in the 1950s.[8]

Although Sam Shepard might say about Duarte what he once wrote about Plymouth, Massachusetts, that it is "the kind of place you aspire to get out of the second you dis-

6. *Motel Chronicles*, pp. 17–19.
7. Ibid., p. 14.
8. Ibid., p. 86.

cover you've had the misfortune to have been raised there,"[9] he did come into contact with things that had a positive effect on his art. One of these was his father's music. Sam Sr. was an amateur musician, a drummer in a local Dixieland band. He had an extensive record collection of American popular music, which helped give Steve a good background in jazz forms, though at the time he was getting it, he hated his father's music. Steve Rogers too became a drummer and later, as Sam Shepard, joined the Holy Modal Rounders. More importantly, music came to occupy a significant place in his plays, at times even appearing to dominate language. In an interview printed in a 1974 issue of *Theatre Quarterly* Shepard made some strong claims for music: "I think music's really important, especially in plays and theatre—it adds a whole different kind of perspective, it immediately brings the audience to terms with an emotional reality. Because nothing communicates emotions better than music, not even the greatest play in the world."[10]

At first the music that influenced Shepard was jazz, an influence that stemmed partly from his childhood, but more directly from his early experiences in New York. Later, he came to reject jazz in favor of rock and roll, moving to England in 1971 partly in hope of getting into a rock group like The Who. In *Hawk Moon* Shepard made the definitive statement about the power that rock and roll exercised over him and, as he saw it, over our time:

> Rock and Roll is definitely a motherfucker and always will be Rock and Roll made movies theatre books painting and art go out the window none of it stands a chance against The Who The Stones and old Yardbirds Credence Traffic The Velvet Underground Janis and Jimi and on and on . . . Rock and Roll gets it on better than football baseball even boxing . . .

9. Sam Shepard, *Rolling Thunder Logbook* (New York: The Viking Press, 1977), p. 24.

10. Kenneth Chubb and the editors of *Theatre Quarterly*, "Metaphors, Mad Dogs, and Old Time Cowboys," reprinted in *American Dreams: The Imagination of Sam Shepard*, edited by Bonnie Marranca (New York: Performing Arts Journal Publications, 1981), p. 201.

Rock and Roll is violence manifest without hurting no one
. . . Rock and Roll is more revolutionary than revolution.[11]

In Duarte, Shepard also had his first contact with modern literature. He read the beat writers Jack Kerouac, Gregory Corso, and Lawrence Ferlinghetti, and, as Shepard has described it, had a copy of Samuel Beckett's *Waiting for Godot* thrust on him by a guy "who was called a beatnik by everybody in the school because he had a beard and he wore sandals."[12] Although he didn't understand the play, and perhaps didn't even have the sense that it was a play, he claims to have read it with real interest. Shepard rejects the idea that the play became a model for him, but he did admit that after reading it he was forcefully struck with the idea "that with words you could do *anything*."[13]

Sam Shepard did not immediately become a writer. He tried but admits that what he wrote "was pretty bad." He even wrote a play during this time, a Tennessee Williams imitation about a girl who gets raped in a barn. As he approached the end of his high school years, however, it seemed more likely that he would become a veterinarian. To an interviewer's question regarding his feelings about moving to Duarte, he replied: "I really liked being in contact with animals and the whole agricultural thing. . . . And I had a chance actually to manage a sheep ranch, but I didn't take it. I wanted to do something like that, working with animals. I even had the grand champion yearling ram at the Los Angeles County Fair one year."[14]

When it finally came down to it, Shepard chose escape over managing a sheep ranch. And quite accidentally, as he put it, he chose the theater as his escape route. Seeing an ad in a newspaper, he auditioned for a traveling stock company called Bishop's Company Repertory Players and was hired. He was on the road again.

For six months Shepard toured the country playing a

11. *Hawk Moon*, p. 55.
12. Chubb, "Metaphors," p. 191.
13. Quoted in Pete Hamill, "The New American Hero," *New York Magazine*, 5 December 1983, p. 86.
14. Chubb, "Metaphors," pp. 188, 189.

variety of one night stands, mostly to church groups. Not much information is available about this period, except that Shepard considers the religious character of the performances to have been a phony cover for a group of actors who had no other outlets for their ambition. It was also during this time that Samuel Shepard Rogers, Jr., began to call himself Sam Shepard, a name change that he says brought some consternation to his family since the name had gone on for seven generations. Later, in one of the most autobiographical of his plays, *The Holy Ghostly*, Shepard uses the changing of a given name as a point of conflict between a father and son and as a definite sign of the son's rejection of his family background. "I know ya' set out to hurt me," says the father. "Right from the start I knowed that. Like the way ya' changed yer name and all. That was rotten. . . . That name was handed down for seven generations, boy."

In 1963, at age nineteen, Shepard landed in New York. Having no place to go and no particular plan for what he wanted to do, he wandered around until he learned that a high school friend of his, Charlie Mingus, Jr., son of the great jazz musician, was working as a waiter at the Village Gate, one of the most prominent of the New York jazz clubs. Soon Shepard was working there as a busboy, earning fifty dollars a week "cleaning up dishes and bringing Nina Simone ice." The Gate provided Shepard with more than a livelihood. Every night he heard the best of American jazz artists, whose music influenced the style and structure of his early plays. He also met Ralph Cook, who, in addition to being the headwaiter at the Gate, had founded the Theatre Genesis at St. Mark's in the Bowery. Under the influence of the beat poets, Shepard had been writing poetry; Cook encouraged him to try writing for the theater also.

In the early sixties the Off Off Broadway movement was just getting underway. Broadway had long been closed to anything new, and even Off Broadway, so important to New York theatrical life, had become another establishment, largely unsympathetic to the kind of playwrights who had created it. The response was a new theater movement that operated out of church basements, store fronts, small cafes, and lofts, which became the proving ground for a new generation of playwrights.

Sam Shepard arrived in New York at just the right time. Not long before, there had been no Theatre Genesis, Judson Poets Theatre, Cafe La Mama, American Place Theatre, Cafe Cino, or Open Theatre. The culture of New York's East Village, where most of the Off Off Broadway activity was centered, provided a fertile field in which new artistic endeavor could grow. It also provided an open, accepting, and inexpensive living environment necessary to keep the artists themselves alive. Ten years later Shepard described this time and place: "On the Lower East Side there was a special sort of culture developing. You were so close to the people who were going to the plays, there was really no difference between you and them—your own experience was their experience, so that you began to develop that consciousness of what was happening. . . . I mean nobody knew what was happening, but there was a sense that something was going on. People were arriving from Texas and Arkansas in the middle of New York City, and a community was being established. It was a very exciting time."[15]

The exciting time for Shepard included both living and writing. He moved into an East Village apartment on Avenue C with Charlie Mingus, Jr., and jazz drummer Danny Richmond. Along with Mingus, Shepard prowled the streets and played cowboys and Indians. "People stared . . . at him," wrote Patti Smith in a different but similar context: "he didn't care / he was a renegade with nasty habits / he was a screech owl / he was a man playing cowboys."[16]

Out of this youthful energy and role-playing came Shepard's first play, *Cowboys*. It was written quickly and with little rewriting, emerging almost intuitively as a transcription of the role-playing. A comment he made fourteen years later reveals clearly the creative impulse from which

15. Ibid., p. 193.
16. Smith, "Sam Shepard," p. 242.

this play emerged: "The reason I began writing plays was the hope of extending the sensation of *play* (as in 'kid') on into adult life."[17] Although no copies of *Cowboys* have survived, the play impulse exists in other early works, especially *Cowboys #2*, a 1967 rewrite of the original *Cowboys*.

The prominence of the cowboy in Shepard's work reflects a romanticized image of the West more than the actuality of history. That is not to say that Shepard is naive about the true nature of the West or of the cowboy. Rather, he chooses to emphasize the mythic qualities of this figure, which he finds to be both personally and culturally important. When asked why cowboys appear in many of his plays, his response revealed a youthful identification with them and an attraction to their wandering life-style: "Cowboys are really interesting to me . . . most of them really young, about 16 or 17, who decided they didn't want to have anything to do with the East Coast, with that way of life, and took on this immense country, and didn't have any real rules. Just moving cattle, from Texas to Kansas City, from the North to the South, or wherever it was." Continuing his explanation, he implied a comparison between the camaraderie of cowboys on a trail ride and his relationship with Charlie Mingus as they ran around together in New York, contrasting the freedom of their lifestyle with "all these people who were going to work and riding the buses."[18] Later, Shepard would question the hold that the cowboy figure had on his imagination and the effect it was having on his writing, but in 1963 and for some time after, the cowboy provided a necessary artistic impetus.

With his first play now written, Shepard contacted Ralph Cook, who not only had been the one to encourage him in the first place but who also had the means to produce the play. Cook agreed to stage it, and on 10 October 1964 *Cowboys* premiered at the Theatre Genesis on a double bill with another Shepard one-act play, *The Rock Garden*. Initial reviews were so bad that Shepard considered re-

17. Sam Shepard, "Language, Visualization, and the Inner Library," in *American Dreams*, p. 214.
18. Chubb, "Metaphors," p. 190.

turning to California. Then, Michael Smith, drama critic for the *Village Voice*, gave the plays a rave review, and the entire prospect for Shepard changed.

At that period the *Village Voice* exercised an authority on artistic matters for its readership unparalleled by any other New York newspaper. In a sense the *Voice* was guardian of what was new and experimental in the New York art scene, especially for that part of it located in Greenwich Village and its surroundings. When the *Voice* spoke, its readers listened, often for good reason. Time has shown, as it has often done for *Voice* opinions, that Michael Smith was correct. Something was happening at the Theatre Genesis that demanded attention, and as people continued to go, they were rewarded by the originality and energy of the first utterances of a major voice in American theatre.

As *Cowboys* expressed the freedom and independence Shepard felt in New York, *The Rock Garden* recorded his rebellion against his past. It was his first play about the American family and, to some degree, about his own family and his leaving home. The play aroused some controversy because of the overt sexual content of the monologue that ends it. In 1967 this monologue was incorporated into Kenneth Tynan's revue *Oh! Calcutta!*

The Rock Garden has a striking but simple structure. It is composed of three scenes, the first of which sets the tone of the action and establishes the essential alienation of the family members. A boy and a girl, both teenagers, sit opposite each other at a dinner table. They are sipping from glasses of milk and exchanging glances. At the head of the table, thoroughly engrossed in reading a magazine, sits a man. He does not acknowledge the presence of the boy and girl, nor do they acknowledge him. The gulf that separates them appears to be unbridgeable. After a long silence, the girl spills her milk and the scene blacks out. The absence of dialogue, the nameless anonymity of the characters, the utter banality of the simple and isolated actions, and the total lack of contact between the teenagers and the man join to form an image of family life that already incorporates the meaning developed more elaborately in the subsequent scenes.

Scene 2 introduces a new character, identified only as the woman. She is lying on a bed, and the boy, dressed only in underwear, is seated in a rocking chair. The man and the girl are not present. The woman discusses her father, who kept an attic full of cats and would spend days alone with them, separated from his family. She then talks about her husband, complaining repetitively that he won't do certain things like puttying the drafty windows, even though he does physical labor all the time in the fields. She also compares the boy both to her father and to his father, identifying common physical characteristics. During the course of her speeches she asks the boy to bring her glasses of water and blankets. Each time the boy returns with the requested thing, he is wearing an additional piece of clothing until he appears fully dressed. At that point, the man enters wearing a hat and overcoat, and the boy runs off stage. The man exits and then reenters dressed only in underwear. The man takes the boy's place in the rocking chair, as he has already replaced him in terms of dress, and the scene ends.

Scene 3 most strongly picks up the separation theme introduced in scene 1. The man and the boy are both seated, the man on a couch downstage and the boy on a chair facing upstage. This time they are both in underwear. Most of the conversation occurs in two monologues, the first one delivered by the father, in which he talks about the lawn, the fence, his rock garden, and their farm's orchard and irrigation system. His descriptions are tediously repetitive, and the boy periodically nods off from boredom and falls out of his chair. When the man finishes, the boy launches into a graphic description of his sexual preferences and practices, at the end of which the man falls off the couch. The boy's monologue is as startling and personal as the man's is banal and impersonal. It is an aggressive response to all that is no longer bearable in the boy's home life, especially to the tedium of uncommunicative relationships; the man for example does not notice when the boy falls off his chair, just as in scene 1 he never looked from behind his magazine and did not see the girl spill her milk.

Although Shepard has said that *The Rock Garden* is about

leaving his mother and father,[19] the setting, action, and characters are deliberately generalized, suggesting that the condition it describes is a common one. Many of the plays he wrote after this also concern the problem of the family, of individuals attempting to survive as individuals within a group that demands, if it is to be successful, a high degree of cooperation, love, and selflessness. In every case, however, there is a failure of this nuclear community as its members prey on each other and seek to dominate.

Cowboys and *The Rock Garden* were another rite of passage for Shepard. In them he had taken leave of his family and played out a ritual of his imagination, using a childhood fascination with cowboys as a vehicle to the world of professional theater. Although limited in its aspiration, *The Rock Garden* is a fully realized work, remarkable for the boldness and clarity of its form as much as for the uninhibited description of its final monologue. Like the work of the absurdist playwrights, it successfully sustains a level of abstraction that substitutes a modernist concern with structure and the primacy of language for traditional notions of character and action. In light of Shepard's background, which gives no obvious explanation of either his talent for writing or this particular literary orientation, *The Rock Garden* is also an unexpected accomplishment. His earlier contact with the work of the Beat writers and Samuel Beckett and his arrival in New York at a propitious time do not sufficiently explain this almost effortless theatrical debut. Obviously, he was ready to accomplish what he did, and whatever the exact confluence of conditions and events, the indifferent student, the teenage renegade, the dreamer of escapes had joined a select fraternity. He had become a writer.

19. Chubb, "Metaphors," p. 193.

II. The Inner Library: Holy
Ghosts Come Home to Roost

"All Sam's plays use the stage to project images," wrote Michael Smith; "they do not relate to the spectator by reflecting outside reality."[1] These images often have their source in the past and emerge with a biting humor born out of irony. They are like X rays of an inner landscape, lacking in shading and color but giving the sharp outlines of a consciousness that examines and reexamines everything and that perpetually puts itself in perspective. The real subject of the plays, therefore, is Shepard's own consciousness, and the outside realities exist only as they have been transformed by consciousness.

The Rock Garden exhibits these subjective qualities, as did *Cowboys*, if *Cowboys #2* can be taken as an accurate representation of the original play. The three plays that Shepard wrote next, however, *Up to Thursday*, *Dog*, and *Rocking Chair*, may not have succeeded in rendering this inner landscape. None of them were ever published, and Shepard himself seems to have largely forgotten them. *Up to Thursday*, produced by Theatre 65, Shepard has called "a bad exercise in absurdity . . . a terrible play, really." It apparently had four people on stage who constantly kept moving their legs and a kid "sleeping in an American flag . . . wearing a jockstrap." The other two were produced at La Mama Experimental Theatre Club: *Dog* was about a black man sitting on a park bench and was influenced by Edward Albee's *Zoo Story*; *Rocking Chair*, which Shepard barely remembers, was, as he put it, "about somebody in a rocking chair." These casual descriptions Shepard has justified by saying, "I find it hard to remain with a certain attachment to things that I wrote. . . . I always feel like

1. Michael Smith, "Notes on *Icarus's Mother*," in Sam Shepard, *Chicago and Other Plays* (New York: Urizen Books, 1967), p. 26.

14

leaving behind rather than hanging on to them."[2]

In April 1965 Theatre Genesis staged Shepard's sixth play, *Chicago*. Unlike the three that immediately preceded it, *Chicago* is a genuine expression of the inner landscape. The entire action exists in relation to the central character, Stu, who spends the whole play in a bathtub placed at center stage. From him flows an almost continuous commentary on the other characters and their actions, as well as a series of imaginative evocations of other places and times. Action that does not directly involve Stu takes place offstage and only becomes audible to the audience when Stu acknowledges it. Stu, then, is more than a character; he is almost a creator of the play. His function is auctorial, and about him on the stage move the projections of his own imagination. As a result, outside reality is essentially banished. The bathtub is in the middle of a bare stage, and the offstage spaces suggest rooms only because of the actions that the dialogue assigns to them. Off right the other characters eat biscuits, implying a kitchen, and off left a phone rings. The absence of any room definition on the stage, however, abstracts the offstage spaces and locates them subjectively in Stu's consciousness. The actions of the main body of the play are further separated from reality and defined as theatrical renderings by three loud knocks of a policeman's club on the back of a chair at the rear of the theater, which occur at the beginning and end of the play.

The first spoken lines of *Chicago* are from the Gettysburg Address, read very loudly through the theater's sound system. The curtains open, revealing Stu sitting in his bathtub delivering, in a singsong manner, a free-association wordplay monologue. As Stu continues, the Gettysburg Address fades out, allowing the two speeches to blend into each other and suggesting that the concepts of liberty and equality that are at the heart of Lincoln's speech will be relevant to the play. The imaginative nature of Stu's "song" immediately sets him apart from the other main character,

2. Chubb, "Metaphors," p. 194.

Joy, who is concerned with the more mundane question of the biscuits she has been making. She calls persistently to Stu to come and get some. When he finally stands in order to leave the bathtub, it is revealed that he is wearing long pants and tennis shoes even though he is unclothed from the waist up. This revelation further removes the bathtub from the realm of everyday reality and prepares us for Stu's next flight of fancy, a description of being on the beach that is partly delivered in the voice of an old woman chastising young female bathers for their flimsy bathing suits and high, mighty, and flashy attitudes. Joy's response is a down-to-earth "Fuck off!," prompting Stu to ask, "Who needs biscuits at this hour? Who ever needs biscuits?"

After this remark, a phone call reveals that another woman, Myra, is coming over and that Joy has gotten a job somewhere that will make it necessary for her to leave. Never is there any sense that Stu has a job, so that Joy's having one places her even more firmly in the nonimaginative world. Nevertheless, after the phone call, she gets in the tub with Stu and imagines the tub as a boat with fish swimming in the water around them. Stu, however, changes the terms of this imagemaking by telling Joy that the fish are barracuda and that they want to eat her. He tries to force her out of the tub and into the "water." Joy struggles to stay in the tub but is only saved because Myra arrives and the conversation turns to more normal matters.

Now out of the tub, Joy returns to her preparations for leaving. Stu, on the other hand, not only remains in the tub but continues his imaginative play with the idea of fish. He addresses the fish directly and describes how fishermen will set out to catch them, rowing out to the middle of the lake and dropping their hooks, breaking out their thermos bottles of coffee and pea soup while they wait, and how the fish will swim around the hook cautiously, hungry but not sure whether to take the worm. The fishermen meanwhile will discuss how nice the fish heads would look mounted over their fireplaces, and they will be "grinning and pointing at the moon and the pier and all the trees." Early in the monologue Stu admonishes the fish not to "just hang there treading water," advice that would

16

just as well apply to the fishermen. "You're both hung up," Stu finally concludes, a remark that defines the condition of all the other characters in the play.

As Stu finishes this monologue, the phone rings again. Joy answers and invites Joe to come over. When Joy reenters, she is carrying a fishing pole, a prop which from this point all the other characters will arrive carrying. This clearly relates them to the fishermen of Stu's story, implying that they too are hung up, and unable to make an imaginative move. In addition, they all dress alike and become enthusiastically involved in the biscuit eating. At the end of the play, they sit on the edge of the stage and cast their fishing lines into the audience, suggesting that if they are like the fishermen, the audience must be like the fish, also hung up, involved in a standoff, hungering for some kind of liberty but unable to take the imaginative step that will get them there.

As the play moves toward its conclusion, Stu delivers three more monologues. The first concerns a train trip that becomes transformed by some basic bodily functioning. Stu's scatological language contrasts sharply with Joy's properly dressed, biscuit-eating friends. As the train passengers fall asleep, Stu describes "a cowboy picking his teeth and spitting little gobs of food into the aisle" and then a fat man "farting . . . big windy farts that sort of make a whizzing sound." The fat man finally makes a whole car smell, a smell that "gets into the seats and the pillows and the rug." Stu's direct, unhypocritical language is similar to that used by the boy in *The Rock Garden*, although in this case it is directed toward the audience since no other characters are present when he delivers the monologue. In both cases, of course, it is the audience's sensibility that is assaulted, though in *Chicago* it is done without the mediating device of a character as listener.

The second monologue constructs an elaborate story of the progressive civilizing of a community that leads ultimately to extinction. Once again Stu does not temper his language or his image, and in this case his monologue grows directly out of a confrontation with another character. After complaining that the others are "a bunch of sis-

17

sies . . . pantywaists . . . faggots prancin' around," Stu recounts a parable about a group of sailors who come to
shore "horny for the young virgins that walk the beaches
. . . screwing everything in sight." Years pass and they are
still at it, their boats now rotting away on the beach. Babies
are born, and up and down the beach men and women lay
in mounds, their bodies covered in sperm and sand, their
hair growing all over. Night comes and they build fires;
they continue by the fires, "picking each other's nose,"
licking each other, purring and farting "all they want to."
Then a change takes place. They move away from the
beach and build a house on the side of a hill. They begin
making rugs until the whole house is covered with them.
Finally, they can no longer breathe because there are so
many rugs, so they begin to scream and claw at each other.
At last they come out and one by one walk down to the
beach and into the water "until you can't see them any
more."

At the conclusion of this monologue, the others come on
as a group to bid Joy goodbye. She backs off pulling a wa-
gonload of suitcases, and the group go to the edge of the
stage with their fishing poles and cast into the audience.
They sit there gazing ahead, the ultimate products of a
civilizing tendency, hung up on their conventionality and
their insipid lack of imagination.

At this point Stu begins his final monologue by continuing the beach metaphor. Using the second person pronoun
you, he addresses the audience, though at first he is unseen because he is lying back in the tub. He creates an
image of the "you" walking slowly on the beach and sweat-
ing, looking out across the milk-white sea to a whole town
of lights on the other side. The slow movement gives way
to a more rapid one, and the walkers' breathing increases.
As Stu reaches this place in his description, he jumps out
of the bathtub, walks to the edge of the stage, and talks to
the audience directly, encouraging them to breathe deeper.
"The place is teeming with air," he exclaims. "All you do is
breathe. Easy. . . . Before your very eyes. Outstanding air.
All you need to last a day. Two days. A week. Month after
month of breathing until you can't stop. Once you get the

taste of it. The hang of it. What a gas. . . . Ladies and gentlemen, it's fantastic!" While he is delivering this speech, the actors begin to follow his advice, until they are all breathing in unison. After the elaborate descriptions of the nature of the social and personal illness, Stu's remedy is quite simple, an affirmation of life, fundamentally physical and active, presented by means of an energetic and striking metaphor imaginatively developed.

Chicago was an important step forward for Shepard. It demonstrated that the promise inherent in *Cowboys* and *The Rock Garden* was real and that Shepard was capable of a more complex development of the theatrical ideas he had begun working with in the first two plays, especially the use of spare, antiillusionist settings, distanced and nonengaging characters and action, and the verbal power of the monologue. He expanded the space of action by use of the offstage area as a location for dialogue and by the narrative character of the monologues. The setting moves beyond Stu's bathtub into imaginative worlds of extended metaphor that develop the play's themes in broad cultural and philosophical terms. Unlike *Cowboys* and *The Rock Garden*, which are anchored in Shepard's immediate youthful experiences, *Chicago* reveals a more mature and universal perspective in which the implied social criticism of the earlier plays becomes overt.

The more Shepard wrote, the more he threw himself into writing. As late as 1977 he said, "I write fast because that's the way it happens with me. . . . When I start, I don't stop. Writing is born from a need. A deep burn. If there's no need, there's no writing."[3] The need must have existed from the very beginning, for by the end of 1965, Shepard had put two more plays before the public, *Icarus's Mother* at the Cafe Cino and *4-H Club* at Theatre 65. After little more than a year as a practising playwright, Shepard had eight produced plays to his credit and had become one of the best known of the Off Off Broadway writers.

The first production of *Icarus's Mother* was directed by Michael Smith, whose review of *Cowboys* and *The Rock Gar-*

3. "Language, Visualization, and the Inner Library," p. 218.

den in the *Village Voice* had been instrumental in launching Shepard's career. Although he had trouble with the production and concluded that "it is terribly difficult to produce," he also felt that it was "the best of Sam's plays to date—the fullest, densest, most disturbing and provocative."[4] Others, too, have seen *Icarus's Mother* as disturbing and provocative. Critic Michael Bloom found in the play "a pervasive fear that transmits a powerful gestalt to the audience,"[5] and a British interviewer was prompted to ask Shepard about "the almost political sense of an outside threat" that it contains. Shepard himself traced some of this quality to a Fourth of July celebration that he had once attended in Milwaukee: "One of the weird things about being in America now . . . is that you don't have any connection with the past, with what history means; so you can be there celebrating the Fourth of July, but all you know is that things are exploding in the sky. And then you've got this emotional thing that goes a long way back, which creates a certain kind of chaos, a kind of terror, you don't know what the fuck's going on. . . . There's a vague kind of terror going on, the people not really knowing what is happening."[6] In 1975, while traveling with Bob Dylan's Rolling Thunder Revue, Shepard noted a similar feeling accompanying the preparations for the Bicentennial. "New England is festering with Bicentennial madness," he wrote in *Rolling Thunder Logbook*, "as though desperately trying to resurrect the past to reassure ourselves that we sprang from somewhere. A feeling that in the past at least there was some form or structure and that our present state of madness could be healed somehow by ghosts."[7]

Icarus's Mother opens calmly enough. Bill, Pat, Howard, Jill, and Frank are lying on the grass after having a picnic. They are watching a jet that has been flying overhead for an hour, speculating on the pilot's motives, wondering if his vapor trail is meant to be a signal. Bill, finding the pres-

4. Smith, "Notes on *Icarus's Mother*," p. 26.
5. Michael Bloom, "Visions of the End: The Early Plays," in *American Dreams*, p. 75.
6. Chubb, "Metaphors," pp. 195–96.
7. *Rolling Thunder Logbook*, p. 45.

ence of the plane "distracting," yells at the pilot to go away. The vagueness of the anxiety that the plane produces in Bill is expressed in his line: "We don't know what you want but we don't want you around here!" The others, however, are more open and yell for the pilot to land. Jill and Pat even pretend to be the pilot's wife and try to coax him down with implied sexual promises. Bill, too, joins in this game. The plane leaves, however, and the group turn to a discussion of what to do before the fireworks start. Pat says she wants to walk on the beach, but the others try to dissuade her, first by saying that she might miss the fireworks and then by suggesting that she might fall and get hurt. Finally, it is Frank who leaves first in order to find a place to "pee." Then, Jill and Pat go off for a walk, leaving Bill and Howard behind. Frank returns with a glowing description of the beach and how fantastic it is. He tries to convince Bill and Howard to move down to the beach to see the fireworks, but they are not interested. When Frank suggests an exploring party to "find out what there is to know about the beach," Bill responds that "there's nothing to know." He then proves his statement by giving a textbook definition of a beach. Like Joy's friends in *Chicago*, Bill and Howard are not capable of the imaginative response that Frank, a character more like Stu, has. Frank leaves again, this time in search of Jill and Pat.

While the others are gone, Bill and Howard begin sending smoke signals by alternately covering and uncovering their portable barbeque with the picnic tablecloth; each time the others return, though, Bill and Howard stop what they are doing and try to get rid of the intruders. Their anxious signaling activity gets them nowhere, however, while Pat and Jill's more càsual activity on the beach—both crouch down to pee "like a couple of desert nomads or something"—allows them to make contact with the pilot, who flies low over their heads. Once again they coax him sexually, and as a result he climbs to a high altitude and writes, "E equals MC squared" with his vapor trail.

Jill and Pat leave again and Frank returns, this time with the news that the plane has crashed and that Bill and Howard have missed the most spectacular fireworks of all. He then describes the crash in terms that would be appropriate for a nuclear explosion: "blowing itself up six inches above sea level . . . lighting up the air with a gold tint and a yellow tint and smacking the water so that waves go up to five hundred feet. . . . Exploding the water for a hundred miles in diameter around itself. Sending a wake to Japan. An eruption of froth and smoke and flame blowing itself up over and over again."

This apocalyptic ending need not be read in terms of the threat of nuclear destruction. The characters' attempts to control the mysterious pilot and the volatile energy that is expressed in his flying display can also be interpreted sexually. They had come to see a fireworks display, itself a sexual metaphor. Bill remarks that last year's display "was a joke." Howard seconds that opinion with his suggestive line: "fifteen hundred of them exploded before they even got off the launching pad. They just made a little pop, and a stream of smoke came out, and that was it." Pat and Jill are not turned off by this threat of impotence, however. Pat says she will wait all night if necessary because "it's worth it just to see one beautiful one out of all the duds." If necessary she will even "fire the thing without any help and run back up here and lie on my back and wait and listen and watch the goddam thing explode all over the sky."

In this context the appearance of the plane is a promise of a less controllable, more dangerous, and certainly more potent sexuality. When Pat and Jill were on the beach, they took the risk of inviting the pilot by means of their own sexual display. "We started rolling in the sand and showing him our legs. Then we did some of those nasty dances like they do in bars. Then we both went nuts or something and took off our pants and ran right into the water yelling and screaming and waving at his plane." In response to them, the pilot did "flips and slides with that jet like you've never seen before."

The ultimate sexual metaphor is, of course, the crash of the plane. After having soared to a high altitude in response to Pat and Jill's provocation, it plunges toward the sea "passing cloud after cloud and picking up its own speed under its own momentum, out of control." The result is a colossal orgasmic explosion, perhaps best epitomized by the line already quoted: "An eruption of froth and smoke and flame blowing itself up over and over again." The orgasm/crash is so powerful that it consumes the pilot, who is last seen "bobbing in the very center of a ring of fire that's closing in" until at last "the fire moves in and covers him up."

Frank's description of the crash causes a reaction in Bill and Howard that echoes the reaction that the man in *The Rock Garden* had to the boy's monologue. As Frank staggers offstage at the end of his account, Howard and Bill are left facing the audience and holding hands. Jill rushes on and tries to get them to go with her to look at the crash. Howard responds by yelling, "Get away from here!," to which Bill adds, "Get away from the picnic area!" Their refusal to even look at the crash is an extreme rejection of what the pilot and his plane represent. At the same time, their signaling to the plane seems to indicate the opposite but complementary desire to embrace it.

In contrast to their response is that of the crowds of people that Frank said witnessed the crash with a kind of fearful fascination. As the plane blows itself up "over and over again, . . . the community comes out to see for itself. Till the houses open because of the light, they can't sleep. . . . And the porches are filled with kids in pajamas on top of their fathers shielding their eyes. And their mothers hold their fathers with their mouths open. . . . The kids climb down and run to the beach with their mothers chasing and their fathers chasing. . . . And the tide breaks open and the waves go up." Then, as the pilot becomes engulfed in the ring of fire, the crowd of two hundred "bow their heads and moan together with the light in their faces."

The crowd's giving in to their fascination does not result in their destruction, despite the cataclysmic nature of the crash. Rather, it makes them part of a unifying ritual similar to the sexual couplings on the beach described by Stu in *Chicago*, and prefiguring the more spiritual unification that takes place in the Hopi ritual that ends Shepard's later play *Operation Sidewinder*. Jill's final pleading with Bill and

Howard to look at the crash affirms the positive nature of the event. "Everybody's down there!," she exclaims. "It's fantastic." When they still refuse, Jill responds, "All right. But you guys are missing out."

In this light the circling plane, though it certainly stimulates anxiety, is not itself a destructive force. On the contrary, the plane's appearance and its ultimate crash are life-giving elements. They transform the empty ritual of picnic and fireworks, in which most of the fireworks do not even go off, into a new ritual with its own fireworks, which are, as Frank describes them, "something to behold . . . the nineteenth wonder of the Western, international world . . . for the preservation of historians to come and for historians to go by." That the pilot is consumed in the crash in no way contradicts this reading. Before diving for the sea, he had written his own epitaph with the vapor trail of his plane, "E equals MC squared." His crash, therefore, results not in destruction but in transformation from matter into energy. The mass/energy equivalency, of course, puts us on the threshold of nuclear disaster, but in Shepard's play the only things that are threatened are the conventionalized rituals of old forms, and the energy that destroys them brings on a new light. In the world of post-Einstein physics, Icarus's ambitious flight takes on new meaning.

These considerations suggest another way of thinking about the plane and its mysterious pilot. If we can link the anxiety expressed in *Icarus's Mother* to the Bicentennial madness that Shepard described in *Rolling Thunder Logbook*, then the pilot's airborne maneuvers can be compared to the journey that the Rolling Thunder Revue was making. As Shepard explained it, "Rolling Thunder is searching for something too. Trying to make connections. . . . We're looking for ourselves in everything. . . . Trying to locate ourselves on the map. In time and space. . . . What is this whole thing about? Is it a spiritual sojourn of some kind? . . . What in the fuck are we doing out here in blind America looking for a hotel room? . . . The past is this moment escaping."[8] These questions are, of course, the ques-

8. Ibid., p. 45.

tions of an artist trying to define what another group of artists is doing, that is, trying to define art itself. For it is one of the functions of art to make connections and through these connections to define the reality of our experience, in such a way as to shatter the blockages that prevent us from recognizing what that reality is. If that reality is a kind of madness, it certainly cannot "be healed somehow by ghosts," and sometimes it can only be healed by an aggressive attack on the rigidities of outmoded forms, an attack that shocks its target into new perceptions. It is the artist in this circumstance who is the aggressor. In *Icarus's Mother*, then, the plane and its pilot can be seen as a metaphor for the artist and the artistic process. The plane's appearance becomes the catalyst for various responses as it disrupts the normal flow of events and challenges conventional modes of thinking. At his most aggressive, the artist is an aesthetic terrorist.

In the December 1977 issue of the *Drama Review* Shepard described what he called "the inner library," a collection of images gathered from experience that have been stored away in the mind and that can be drawn upon and reused as living sensations and not just as information. He has drawn on these images throughout his career, and often they have been the seeds from which the plays have germinated. Responding once to an interviewer who seemed surprised when Shepard told him that he wrote, at least in the early days, without planning, he explained, "I would have like a picture, and just start from there. A picture of a guy in a bathtub, or of two guys on stage with a sign blinking—you know, things like that."[9] From these images emerged the plays, and then from the plays—and only then, insisted Shepard—came the ideas. The more traditional critical notion that plays emerge from ideas he has rejected as opposite to his experience.

Although this formulation oversimplifies a complex process, it should by no means be rejected out-of-hand. The inner library is clearly evident in the plays that have been discussed so far: *Cowboys* stemmed directly from the movie

9. Chubb, "Metaphors," p. 191.

image of the cowboy and from Shepard's youthful playing out of the cowboy role; *The Rock Garden* recreated feelings of boredom and the image of his parents locked into unresponsive patterns of thought and conduct; *Chicago* made concrete the absurd image of the guy in a bathtub refusing to join into the normal patterns of activity going on around him; and *Icarus's Mother* rendered that image of chaos and terror that Shepard had encountered at the Fourth of July celebration. A single image, however, does not make a play, and the process of giving context to an image inevitably involves more than just adding other images or expanding the one from which the play was born. The process is the process of ideas, and, therefore, to say that "ideas emerge from plays" is to say that ideas emerge from the writings of plays. Shepard described this working method as the image "moving in the mind and being allowed to move more and more freely as you follow it."[10] Play writing then is following the image, but it is not some kind of vague daydreaming or simply a form of inspiration, any more than it is a direct rendering of the natural and social world. It is imaginative work in which the world is recreated in the image and likeness of the artist. Shepard might join with Whitman in chanting "I celebrate myself, and what I shall assume, you shall assume" or with Blake in warning against the deadly effect of natural objects on the imagination.

Shepard's last play of 1965 seems to have had its source in his first experiences of living in the run-down apartments of the East Village. Ironically titled *4-H Club*, it works from a series of violent images that are conjured up by the play's three male characters. Shepard himself was a member of the 4-H Club during his high school days in Duarte. The only animals in his play, however, are mice, rats, wolverines, and baboons, all of which are talked about as creatures to kill or be killed by. As the men's discussions of these animals, none of which ever actually appear in the play, move from the harmless ones to the dangerous ones, the language becomes more graphically

10. "Language, Visualization, and the Inner Library," p. 215.

violent, depicting, for example, how the baboon dismembers its prey and takes certain portions of the body back to its mate.

Preceding the animal images is much discussion of cleaning up the apartment in which the men live. Near the very beginning of the play, two of the men, John and Bob, smash their coffee cups on the floor and kick the pieces around. The other man, Joe, sweeps up the pieces, only to have them kicked again. At that point Joe delivers a monologue on neatness, although he claims that he doesn't care about neatness but is only concerned that no one gets cut on the broken glass. During this monologue, Joe refers to the audience. He tells John and Bob that if he was only interested in neatness, he could wash the place down with a fire hose, though "it would probably wash the stove out into the audience." For a character to discuss a piece of the stage setting as stage setting, as something that exists in relation to an audience, is to reveal the play as just play and to suggest that all the actions of the characters are to be understood as playacting rather than as mimesis.

The playacting quality is evident throughout *4-H Club*. The three characters react to each other almost as children, even though their images and references are taken from the adult world. When the play begins, John is downstage making coffee, and Bob and Joe are in the kitchen area laughing wildly, with Bob jumping up and down and Joe smacking the floor with a broom. As their laughter grows into hysteria, they begin rolling on the floor. From this point, when one or another of the men tries to be serious, the other two respond with either disruptive actions or imaginative word play. Their conversations are disjunctive as they move rapidly from topic to topic. They invent stories, try to top each other with wilder and more threatening variations on them, stomp around, shout, whisper, and act out the images they create. Their activity is governed only by the flights of fancy they conjure up in the middle of their squalid urban surroundings.

In the culminating image John describes the country in which the baboons live, while Bob wrestles with Joe, who repeatedly bangs the coffeepot on a hot plate: "It's always good weather for some reason. . . . The water is so blue you can see all the way to the bottom. . . . The air smells so good you can taste it. . . . It's a great place. I'm going to do some swimming too. Floating on my back. You just float and stare at the sky." This imaginative projection contrasts sharply with the wrestling and noise going on while John talks. As in *Chicago*, the image of a different experience hangs over the characters and their environment as the play ends, an experience that is enticing though perhaps unreachable except through imagination.

The absurdity of the play's humor and the way in which the dialogue moves from subject to subject by means of association suggests the influence of the great Irish playwright Samuel Beckett. Its language, although sparer than that of *Chicago* and *Icarus's Mother*, has a snap and energy that cannot be found in any of the other surviving plays of this period. It moves with the pacing of a good vaudeville sketch, the actors rapidly trading one-liners, puns, and tall stories, or with the improvisatory changes of a group of jazz musicians jamming. One character, for example, will begin a story with an image, and another will continue it and develop it. Then the first will pick it up again and add another element, the second following along with some variation.

For Shepard, this kind of writing could take on a life of its own. He would get the sense that something in him was doing the writing, a sense that also came to him as a musician when he was playing drums in the Holy Modal Rounders. When Shepard described this sense to Peter Stampfel, one of the founders of the group, Stampfel ascribed it to a visitation by the Holy Ghost, an explanation which Shepard has said "sounded reasonable enough at the time."[11] These visitations that can take the form of writing are related to Shepard's idea of the inner library, the storehouse of images that at any time can spring into the conscious mind as "a living sensation."

Early in 1966 the Firehouse Theatre in Minneapolis produced *Fourteen Hundred Thousand*, one of Shepard's most

11. Ibid., p. 217.

problematic, and yet fascinating, plays. "From a critical point of view," wrote director Sydney Schubert Walter, "the production was undeniably a failure." Shepard, who was present at rehearsals, felt that Walter's staging was subverting the intentions of the play, and Walter felt that Shepard's conceptions would render the play untheatrical. The result was an in-between production that pleased no one.

Later criticism has sometimes bypassed the play completely or given it only short shrift. In a book on Sam Shepard, Arthur Kopit, and the Off Broadway theater, Doris Auerbach gives the play only one paragraph,[12] while an essay by Gerald Weales does not mention it at all, even though it discusses *Chicago*, *Icarus's Mother*, and *Red Cross*, the play that followed *Fourteen Hundred Thousand*.[13] Another essay, Michael Bloom's "Visions of the End," gives significant space to other early plays but allows *Fourteen Hundred Thousand* only two paragraphs, which conclude that "we are bombarded with an array of ideas and concepts that remain unconnected dramatically, making the play an unwieldy theatrical experience."[14]

Fourteen Hundred Thousand is one of Shepard's most radically formal plays. When Sydney Schubert Walter set out to stage it, he purposefully tried to transform the play's formal strategies into more conventional modes. Essentially, he tried to make the play more naturalistic and dynamic, a procedure that could only contradict Shepard's intentions. The play's severe and abstracted set, restricted blocking, schematic use of light changes, and precise delivery of lines alienate the audience from the action and suggest the theatrical theory and practice of Bertolt Brecht, whom Shepard has cited as his "favorite playwright."[15]

At the heart of Brecht's theater was the establishment of a new relationship between audience and play. In an essay entitled "Theatre for Pleasure or Theatre for Instruction,"

12. *Sam Shepard, Arthur Kopit, and the Off Broadway Theater* (Boston: Twayne Publishers, 1982), pp. 14–15.
13. "The Transformations of Sam Shepard," in *American Dreams*, pp. 37–44.
14. Bloom, "Visions of the End," pp. 76–77.
15. Chubb, "Metaphors," p. 202.

Brecht defined this relationship and its meaning quite precisely: "The spectator was no longer in any way allowed to submit to an experience uncritically . . . by means of simple empathy with the characters in the play. The production took the subject matter and the incidents shown and put them through a process of alienation: the alienation that is necessary to all understanding. When something seems 'the most obvious thing in the world' it means that any attempt to understand the world has been given up."[16]

Fourteen Hundred Thousand holds off its audience in this way. Rather than an integrated dramatic action, the audience is confronted with a highly formal structure consisting of recurring actions, simple and clearly defined manipulations of the set, carefully balanced blocking and arrangement of props, and a progressive domination of language over action. Descriptions of the play as untheatrical are really responses to this structural, rather than character/action mode of presentation. It is untheatrical only if one defines theater in terms of what both Shepard and Brecht are rejecting. Like many other modern artists, Shepard is using a technique akin to Brecht's alienation effect, though he uses it for primarily formal rather than didactic purposes and certainly not within Brecht's ideological framework.

Action in *Fourteen Hundred Thousand* is reduced to two components: building a bookcase and entering and exiting through a door. Correspondingly, the set serves these two functions and is made up of a white wall that runs the width of the upstage area, a large unfinished bookcase set against the wall stage right, and a door in the wall stage left. The play begins in medias res with Tom standing on a stool facing the bookcase, hammer in hand and nails in his mouth, and Ed standing in the open doorway. The lights come up rapidly to a bright blue, and Ed delivers the closing lines of an invitation for Tom to visit him somewhere. Ed exits, the lights change rapidly to white, and a shelf

16. Cited in *Brecht on Theatre*, ed. and trans. John Willet (New York: Hill and Wang, 1964), p. 71.

falls off the bookcase. Tom gets off the stool, picks up the shelf, returns it to its original place, and the lights change back to blue. Ed immediately reenters carrying lumber, and Tom begins to speak to him as if he had never left. They discuss a cabin that was given to Ed, which he is in the process of fixing up. Whenever Ed speaks, Tom begins to hammer, and Ed has to yell to be heard. Ed once again invites Tom to spend some time at the cabin and then stands as if to leave. Tom berates him for leaving "in the middle of a job," and Ed responds that he has already built the structure for him and that he also has to finish working on the cabin before it snows. Throughout this conversation, both Tom and Ed have their backs to the audience. Tom makes a final sarcastic remark to Ed about rushing to the aid of his cabin, and a shelf falls off the bookcase again. The lights return to white, and Donna enters carrying cans of white paint and brushes. She sets the cans down and sits on them with her back to the audience. Tom gets off the stool, picks up the shelf, and replaces it.

By this point in the play, the basic structural pattern has been established. While the bookcase is being worked on, the other characters enter and exit carrying things—lumber, paint, books. After putting their items down, they sit on them with backs to the audience. The one working on the shelf also stands with back to the audience and hammers while the others are trying to talk to him, forcing them to yell in order to be heard. On entrances and exits the lights change color, either from blue to white or white to blue, and often shelves fall off the bookcase. These elements repeat until, at a crucial juncture near the end of the play, the actors dismantle the set, leaving the stage entirely bare. Action ceases and the two characters who are left on stage read alternately from a book about city planning.

Shortly after Donna enters with the paint, Ed again says that he has to leave, that he can't stay to see the finished product. Donna responds that there will not be anything in particular to see since the bookcase is just an everyday, functional item. This remark becomes the focal point for all of Tom's frustrations about building the shelf, which in themselves are just symptomatic of a more pervasive frustration with the basic inertness of their lives. Like the man's rock garden in the play of that name, the books are portrayed as lifeless objects, no longer linked to the ideas they contain. Tom berates Donna with the accusation that she never reads the books to begin with, that the ones she has read have only been half read, and that the rest she bought for decorative purposes. "Fourteen hundred thousand books to put in a bookcase once and never touch them again till the day you die," he scolds. Donna responds with a defense of her reading habits and the ultimatum that they will not go on vacation until the shelf is finished, filled with books, "waxed, polished, and smells like the great outdoors!" This last remark is especially significant since it defines one thing in the contradictory terms of another. The shelf and its books become the standard by which all activity is measured; they become an end in themselves rather than a means. Tom even suggests that books should be thrown out once they are read, a notion which is immediately rejected by Ed, who describes the emotional attachment he develops for books, "like you would with a pet dog." To this, Tom responds, "You throw away the book, not the effect."

Whatever the validity of both Tom's and Ed's responses to collecting books, it is Donna's unyielding devotion to them as objects that allows them to function significantly in the play. After her mother trudges in with an armload of books, complaining how heavy they are and how hard it was to carry them up the stairs, Donna justifies her effort: "It's worth it though, Mom. When they're all stacked in and divided into topical categories, it's really a sight to see." Mom's response to this remark puts the whole activity into ironic perspective: "Libraries fascinate me to death."

Death indeed! The reification of people and actions seems an almost inescapable result of social organization in Shepard's America, whether on the scale of the family or of the nation. Just before the boy in *The Rock Garden* falls off his chair for the third time, the man points with pride and a sense of accomplishment to his newest interest: "Did you notice the rock garden? That's a new idea. . . . It's one of those new kind. You know? With rocks and stuff in it. It has lots of rocks and stuff from the trip. We found afterwards that it was really worth carrying all those rocks around. . . . It gives me something to do. It keeps me pretty busy. . . . It's a good feeling. I change it every day. It keeps me busy."

The inanity and redundancy of saying that a rock garden has rocks helps put into perspective the deadly nature of moving the rocks around just to have something to do. In the same way Donna likes to categorize her books, though in her case the results will be even more devastating because they will become "a sight to see," an unchanging collection. As Mom puts it, "Like ancient tapestry or Chinese urns or butterfly collections." At the extreme end of this tendency is some form of extinction, perhaps best expressed in *Chicago* when Stu describes the community that developed out of the mating of the sailors and the beach virgins. As soon as they abandoned the beach and built a house, they began making rugs, at first to keep themselves warm, then for the sake of the rugmaking itself. "They stop screwing, see, and they just make rugs. All day. Years of making rugs until the whole house is covered. . . . They start screaming all together because they can't breathe. They walk across the beach and right into the water. . . . They just keep walking until you can't see them anymore."

Extinction in Shepard is a creeping thing. It comes on slowly and unannounced, turning the familiar into the habitual, people into their activities, and the visible into the invisible, finally swallowing up hopes, promises, and the best of intentions. In *Fourteen Hundred Thousand*, when Tom complains that the others are sitting around watching him, turning him into a show; he gets a response that indicates he is even less than a show. "It's not you in particular," remarks Ed. "It's what you're making." For Ed, and by implication for the others, Tom has disappeared and has been replaced by his activity. In the face of this, Tom's energetic affirmation, "But *I'm* making it! You're watching *me* make *it!*," has no effect. Later in the play, as they discuss Ed's cabin, Donna recalls that her father was once going to build a cabin for them but never did. When she asks him why he let the plan go, he seems not even to remember it. "How could it happen like that?" Donna wonders. "I mean so easily. Without any regrets. . . . Not minding at all one way or the other. Letting things slip away from you as though it didn't matter. As though it were all a joke and talking about a . . . house doesn't really mean there will ever be one."

At this point the repetitive actions of coming and going and of working on the bookcase give way to direct presentation of the ideas through language. Ed suggests that they all go to the cabin in time for the first snow, but instead of taking any action, Mom and Pop use the reference to snow and develop it metaphorically. As if reading from books, they speak in unison: "And the snow started early and came so soft that nobody even noticed." Ed continues to speak about the cabin through the first part of this recitation as if he doesn't hear Mom and Pop, and they in turn go on without reference to what he is saying: ". . . it wouldn't stop and it kept going on. . . . But the funny thing was that there wasn't any wind and there wasn't any cold. It just fell and changed everything from the color it was to white. . . . It got thicker and thicker and covered all their trees." Like the multiplying number of rugs in *Chicago*, the accumulating snow forces the people out of their houses. "It got so bad that they had to climb a hill and watch from the top while their houses disappeared. It happened very slow . . . until the smoke went away from their little chimney tops. . . . They all just looked and didn't say a word but stood in a line looking straight ahead."

During their reading Mom and Pop have been facing front and Tom and Donna have been silently facing the bookcase. Then, as Ed once again tells them he would stay if he could, Tom and Donna join in the recitation about the snow, although they remain facing the bookcase. "The place was in white as far as they could see and not a sound or a wind or a hint of cold or hot. . . . And they moved very slow away from the place." Finally, Ed joins in and all continue in perfect unison. "So they just moved on and on and on. . . . And nobody knows how they ever got lost, how they ever got away. To this very same day nobody knows how they ever got away." On this last line all the shelves on the bookcase fall off.

With the collapse of the shelves and the burying of the cabin and its surroundings under the snow, the play has come to a thematic resolution. It has not come to an aesthetic resolution, however. Up to this point Shepard has created the alienation by means of repeating patterns of action and de-dramatized blocking of the actors. With the exception of Mom and Pop reading, the actors have usually had their backs to the audience, making identification with them almost impossible. In addition, the author has used the sounds of hammering and of the actors shouting over the noise as a distancing device. All these techniques are meant to render the familiar world of human action and the everydayness of the characters' activities unfamiliar and, as a result, to make them more visible. In Brecht's terms, the actions no longer seem "the most obvious thing in the world." On the contrary, they have been defamiliarized, in the sense of the Russian formalists, and the audience, through the very difficulty of the style of presentation, is brought to the state in which understanding the world becomes possible. What in the audience's reality has been covered by the snowstorm of habit and convention is uncovered by the play.

In terms of the play's formal strategies, however, one thing remains to be done. The illusionism of traditional theater has already been challenged; now it must be completely uncovered. As critics have complained, the play is untheatrical, at least in conventional terms. The actors have played with their backs to the audience, action has been made repetitive, and dialogue has been replaced by reading from a text. For Shepard, however, these techniques are precisely theatrical because they make the audience conscious of experiencing theater. In a period when "the subject of painting is seeing . . . the subject of music is hearing . . . the subject of sculpture is space . . . what is the subject of theatre which includes all these and more?," asked Shepard in a brief essay entitled "American Experimental Theatre Then and Now."[17] The answer, of course, is seeing, hearing, and space, and of these three, space is the most important to Shepard. In response to the question of why he wrote plays and not novels or poetry, Shepard said, "I always liked the idea that plays happened in three dimensions, that here was something that came to life in space rather than in a book." The three dimensions of theater, however, are not the same as the three dimensions of life. They are proscribed by the theater itself, by the nature and limits of the stage. For Shepard to complete the distancing of the audience, he had to reveal the space for what it really is. His method in *Fourteen Hundred Thousand* was to have the actors dismantle the set in front of the audience.

At the conclusion of the snow recitation, all the characters except Mom and Pop begin to hum "White Christmas" while they remove the props and dismount the set, carrying everything completely off the stage. As this process goes on, Mom and Pop continue reading, though they introduce a new metaphor for extinction. They begin to compare two conceptions of the city: the traditional radial concept, which "affords certain people who live in certain areas many more benefits and varied ways of living than it does certain other people," and the linear concept, a strip city no more than a mile wide at any point, with "cultural centers . . . evenly distributed along the entire length of the city." At first the linear concept seems to promise a renewal of city life, but as the number of cities multiply, they begin to intersect at right angles, and the amount of space between them begins to dwindle. Finally, cities are built suspended over the other cities, and there are "ocean cities and sky cities and cities underground" until all space in between has been eliminated and another form of extinction has occurred.

In its radical rejection of the usual theatrical elements of characterization, action, identification, drama, and illu-

17. Sam Shepard, "American Experimental Theatre Then and Now," in *American Dreams*, p. 212.

sionism, *Fourteen Hundred Thousand* occupies a unique place in Shepard's body of work. It stands firmly on the side of the theatrical and unyieldingly opposed to the natural. Because it is so purely what it is, it is also representative of much that is essential in Shepard's theater and typical of the formalist tendency of modernist art. As such, it is a paradigm for that aspect of Shepard's art that draws on the aesthetic strategies of Bertolt Brecht and demands a more conscious and intellectual relationship with its audience.

Shepard's next play, *Red Cross*, was first performed at the Judson Poets' Theatre in New York. In several ways, it is similar to *Chicago*: a male character functions as a kind of author/director, imposing his imagination on the other characters; the actors often play to the audience; and the action unfolds in relation to an important prop, in this case twin beds. There are, of course, differences as well: Stu, in *Chicago*, has little effect on the actions of the other characters, while Jim, in *Red Cross*, to a large degree manipulates them, or at least thinks he does; the other characters in *Red Cross* play a more active role than do those in *Chicago*, having important monologues of their own, all of which exhibit the imaginative qualities that are reserved for Stu in *Chicago*; and the set in *Red Cross*, though by no means realistic, is more spatially defined than the one in *Chicago*. Despite the differences, however, both plays are concerned on the formal level with the nature of theatrical performance and make interesting companion pieces to *Fourteen Hundred Thousand*, which denies the presence of the audience and explores the larger questions of theatrical structure and language.

Shepard's stage directions call for a setting in which everything is white, including the costumes, so that when the lights come up, the audience is immediately confronted with this blinding whiteness. For Jacques Levy, who directed the original production, the atmosphere that the setting created demanded a style of performance that also had clarity and definition. In introductory notes to the published play he wrote, "The work of the actors must be sharp and crisp, and I worked toward getting them to slip in and out of character in ways designed to suddenly illuminate a particular facet of what was going on at the moment. And they didn't slowly glide in and out, but (snap!), did it like that—nothing hidden, everything in the clear. . . . The actor thus makes visible that image which relates most closely to what the character is doing, irrespective of whether that character would 'naturally' act in such a way."[18] For example, Carol delivered her monologue about the skiing accident in the style of a radio sportscaster, Jim gave his swimming instructions as if he were an army drill sergeant, and the maid described her feeling of drowning with self-conscious histrionics. Like the presentational mode used in *Fourteen Hundred Thousand*, the techniques and intention of Levy's staging stem from Brecht, particularly from his idea of the "gestic" in acting, a method by which the actor not only expresses a subject but also an attitude toward the subject. In order to achieve this alienation effect, the actor must never "go so far as to be wholly transformed into the character played . . .[but] has just to show the character." The actor then comes between the spectator and the play, short-circuiting the normal process of empathy and freeing "phenomena from that stamp of familiarity which protects them against our grasp."[19]

When the play opens, Carol and Jim are sitting in twin beds, and Carol is complaining about a headache that is so bad that she feels her head is splitting open. She pictures herself skiing and suddenly having the top of her head blown off, sending her crashing down the hill in a frightful tearing up of her body. When she reaches the bottom, it starts snowing and continues until her body is completely covered by "a whole blanket of white snow." After projecting this image of her death, in terms that recall the snow reading in *Fourteen Hundred Thousand*, Carol leaves, reminding Jim that they are to meet at six o'clock.

No sooner is she gone than Jim begins scratching and

18. Jacques Levy, "Notes on *Red Cross*," in *Chicago and Other Plays*, pp. 96–97.

19. Bertolt Brecht, "A Short Organum for the Theatre," in *Brecht on Theatre*, pp. 192–93.

picking crab lice off his legs. A maid enters and starts making the beds. Jim tells her of his lice, and she offers to drive him to a doctor. Instead of going, however, Jim gets the maid to help him change the positions of the beds so that his is now where Carol's used to be. When the maid begins to change the sheets, Jim tries to stop her, implying that he wants Carol to use the crab-infested bed. The maid goes ahead with her changing anyway, telling Jim that the bed no longer is his.

The subject of the beds is now dropped, and Jim tells the maid about swimming at night, suggesting that she try it. She responds that she cannot swim, and Jim proceeds to give her lessons in the room. The beds now become supports for the swimmers, with Jim lying face down on one of them and the maid face down on the other. After a while the maid complains that she is getting cramps in her legs. When Jim urges her to keep going, she reminds him that she is just a beginner, and besides there is no water: "How can I swim on a bed! How can I do it!"

Jim's use of the bed for imaginative play parallels Stu's use of the bathtub in *Chicago*. Unlike *Chicago*, however, it is the maid who takes the play to the next level. As she hobbles around the room holding her side, she describes herself swimming in the lake at night and drowning. Projecting an image of herself underwater, she begins crawling around the room on all fours. Jim now acts like Howard and Bill in *Icarus's Mother* when Frank tells the story of the plane crash. He asks the maid to cut it out, but she responds by keeping the game going and describing herself as turning into a fish. As she comes to the end of her monologue, however, she begins picking up the dirty laundry until she makes a rapid exit from the room.

The maid's monologue, with its taunting quality and its put-on of Jim's seriousness, to some degree shocks Jim out of the self-absorption that is literally eating him alive. He attempts to run after the maid, offering to drive her home, a reversal of the earlier situation in which the maid offered to drive Jim to the doctor, an offer he had to refuse because of its sensibleness. He is stopped, however, by the return of Carol, who at the beginning of the play exhibited her own self-absorption in her severe headache and in the image of her horrible death on the ski slope. She tells Jim that she has bugs all over her body, but he hardly listens as he stares out the screen door of the cabin, still affected by the maid's performance. To Carol's questions, he can only respond with "What?" Although her sharing of the crabs links her to Jim's earlier state, he has in some way been changed by the maid or, at least, has been exposed by the maid. The result of this exposure is registered on Jim not internally but externally in a stream of blood that is seen running down Jim's forehead when he finally turns to look at Carol. Her question, "What happened!," and his response, "When?," indicate that the explanation of the blood has to do with Jim's encounter with the maid and not with some immediate physical cause as is implied in Carol's question.

Crucial to an understanding of the play is the correct reading of the tone of the maid's monologue. One critic sees the play as being apocalyptic, a rendering of contemporary anxiety stemming from the various political, racial, and generational conflicts that surfaced in the 1960s. From this perspective, Carol's skiing image, Jim's crabs, and the maid's "drowning" are "pessimistic visions of impending doom."[20] The problem with this interpretation, however, is that the maid's evocation of her drowning and transformation into a fish is not meant to be taken at face value; rather, it is an extended piece of verbal and visual sarcasm aimed at Jim. The stage direction that Shepard provides for the maid's continued limping around the stage indicates that she "limps more deliberately and holds her side in mock agony." And in one place, in response to Jim's advice on how to deal with the cramp, she says, "It's cramped for good. I'll never swim again." Since she does not know how to swim at all, her line can only be taken sarcastically. The original production emphasized this mocking quality, and as a result the maid's monologue was one of the comic highlights of the play.

The maid's function, then, is to put the other characters

20. Bloom, "Visions of the End," p. 77.

in perspective by ironically turning their absurd visions and sufferings back on themselves. Director Jacques Levy stressed this absurdity by having Jim deliver his "overblown pseudo-soliloquy about his infirmity" as if he were "a jaded, over-the-hill Shakespearean player." In contrast, the maid's monologue was ennobled by her consciously comic attitude toward what she was saying. "When the maid spoke to the audience," wrote Levy, "it became visibly obvious that she had left Jim back in the quagmire of his own making, left him back at the launching pad."[21]

Looking at the play in this way, the apocalyptic gets reduced to something that is more akin to neuroses. Jim and Carol, rather than functioning as agents of Shepard's own pessimism, come to stand for exactly the kind of sensibility that Shepard is criticizing, a sensibility that is born of the idle self-absorption so common to modern American life. The maid, on the other hand, looks outward from the self and through her imaginative performance escapes the quagmire into which Jim is trying to drag her.

The situations, characters, and themes of *Red Cross* led directly into Shepard's next play, *La Turista*, which opened on 4 March 1967 for a limited run at the American Place Theatre in New York City. *La Turista* was Shepard's first full-length play and the first play which he says was rewritten, partly at the request of Jacques Levy, who directed the production, and partly because Shepard was beginning to get the sense of "theatre as an ongoing process." The rewrite resulted in a new second act, which was finished when the play was already in its second week of rehearsals.[22]

The title refers to the form of dysentery that often strikes Americans traveling in Mexico, usually called "Montezuma's Revenge." The play was actually written while Shepard was suffering from the malady himself, an experience he later described in *Motel Chronicles*. At the time, his semi-delirious state apparently caused incoherencies in the second act which, with his health regained, struck him as fill-

21. "Notes on *Red Cross*," p. 97.
22. "Language, Visualization, and the Inner Library," p. 218.

ing the act "with an overriding self-pity." The rewriting became for Shepard a desperate attempt to save the play.[23]

La Turista is a much more complicated play than *Red Cross* not only because it is longer but also because it is richer in associations, references, and ideas. It absorbs *Red Cross*, and for that matter the other early plays, and stands as a summation of Shepard's work to that point. This is not to say that it is necessarily a better play, but only that it is a more ambitious one. For Doris Auerbach this ambition causes the play to be "overburdened with too many concerns and issues, and too many experimental techniques,"[24] but for Elizabeth Hardwick, who wrote the first review of *La Turista*, "the promise of the lofts of off-off Broadway, the dedication and independence, [had] come to the most extraordinary fulfillment."[25]

Once again Shepard confronts his audience with a minimal setting and a shocking use of color. The two beds, occupied by a young couple, have reappeared from *Red Cross*, though the set, instead of being white, is canary yellow and bright orange. Bulging suitcases, signifying the couple's status as tourists, sit at the ends of the beds. Kent, the man, is reading *Time* magazine, and Salem, the woman, is reading *Life*. They are sunburned a bright red and are wearing only underwear. Both their names, taken from brands of cigarettes, and their reading material label them as middle-class Americans.

Throughout their opening dialogue, the characters continue to read as they talk. This alienating device is reinforced by the language of the conversation. They talk about their sunburn but do so in pseudoscientific terms that de-familiarize the subject and allow it to move into a more general discussion of skin color, done in pseudo-anthropological terms and raising the specter of the characters' racial attitudes, an element that runs throughout the first act of the play.

While Kent is in the process of describing what he calls

23. Ibid., p. 218.
24. *Sam Shepard, Arthur Kopit, and the Off Broadway Theater*, p. 16.
25. "Introduction to *La Turista*," in Sam Shepard, *Four Two-Act Plays* (New York: Urizen Books, 1980), p. 13.

fourth-degree burns, a dark-skinned Mexican boy enters carrying a shoeshine kit. Kent immediately assumes that the boy is begging and responds with a strikingly aggressive line that reveals a general attitude toward the boy's culture: "If you weren't so poor, I'd kick you out on your ass. . . . Are they taught by their mothers and fathers to look more despondent than they really are?"

In response to Kent's threat to call the manager, the boy pulls the phone out of the wall and takes it downstage, where he sits and directly confronts the audience. When Kent once again tells the boy to leave, the boy spits in his face. From this point on in the first act, Kent has no more control of the external situation than he has of his internal condition. He rushes to the shower to wash off the spit, only to discover that he is having an attack of "la turista."

While Kent is in the bathroom, Salem tells the boy about an incident in her childhood when her father beat her for spitting. The story suggests that the boy can also be thought of as a son who has done the wrong thing in front of his father. No sooner does Salem finish the story than the phone rings, despite the fact that it has been torn off the wall. The boy answers and speaks to someone who is apparently looking for him. Salem questions the boy about the caller, asking if it is his father. Although she does not get an answer to her question, the question itself reinforces the idea of father/son that the spitting story had implied. Also, as Salem asks her question, Kent is heard calling from the bathroom, so that his call itself becomes a kind of answer. The transformation of boy into son is then made complete, including oedipal overtones when the boy takes off his pants, gets into Kent's bed, and addresses Salem as Mom.

The boy then tells how Mexican ranchers rode into his village, killed his father, and kidnapped his brothers and sisters, forcing them to work twelve hours a day in the fields for a bowl of soup. Salem tells him, "That sounds like a movie," but he ignores her doubt and tells her about a movie he worked in once. His role was to follow the hero, who "wore linen shirts and hand made Campeche boots and one of those straight brimmed Panamanian hats and a pistol with abalone plates on the handle." Ultimately, the hero was devoured by the villagers because someone challenged his image and told him his hat made him look like a clown, thus forcing him to "blow his cool." The boy then confides, again calling Salem Mom, that he wants to be like the movie hero, except that he would not blow his cool, at least not about his hat. "You blow your cool about other shit," he says. "Like when a man spits in your face." At this moment Kent struts in wearing an outfit identical to the movie hero's. The costume links him not only to the hero and, therefore, to the boy who wants to be like him, that is it links Kent and the boy in a variation on the father/son relationship, but also to the hero's fate, a fate which the boy as son instigates by his contempt for the father.

Before Kent is "devoured," he has to play out his role as movie hero. Completely reversing his former image, he expresses contempt for Americans, who have become "a bunch of lily-livered weaklings" because of the excessive cleanliness in the States. He projects a culture that moves more and more toward inbreeding and extinction: "The Greatest Society on its way downhill." His words echo Stu's condemnation of the other characters in *Chicago* and restates the end of the society of rugmakers that Stu evoked in one of his monologues. Ironically, of course, Kent is one of those weaklings. When he sees the boy in his bed, he loses his cool for a second time and faints, never to regain consciousness in the first act.

Salem's reaction is to call a doctor, but the boy suggests some home remedies to counteract poisoning. Ascribing Kent's collapse to the trots, Salem rejects the boy's idea. She runs to the bathroom to get a wet towel, to which the boy replies, "A wet towel is working from the outside in! With poison you have to work from the inside out!" The boy is quite right, of course; Kent has been poisoned by the very things he railed against in his hero speech. The dysentery is only a metaphor for this deeper sickness from which both Kent and Salem suffer.

Almost immediately a knock is heard at the door. A witch doctor and his son enter and proceed to perform a ritual that involves dumping the contents of the suitcases over Kent's body, undressing Kent, setting up candles and burning incense around him, beating him with a rope, and sacrificing two chickens, the blood from which is dripped over Kent's back. As the ritual begins, the boy steps to the edge of the stage to narrate in the manner of an ethnographic film.

The narration functions satirically, like the maid's drowning monologue in *Red Cross*, because its cool anthropological tone contrasts sharply with the ritual itself. It is part of a series of attempts to explain things in a safe way, which include Kent's explanations of sunburn and of the boy's past. The irony of the boy's speech challenges the audience's complacency, especially as the boy's narration becomes more aggressive near its end. He cites two practices that are common in puberty rites, the tearing off of the thumb nail on the right hand and the making of three small incisions with a razor on the end of the penis. Although presented as tribal practices, these are also aggressions of fathers against sons; as such, they are part of the more personal exploration of father/son relationships that can be found not only in this play but throughout Shepard's work.

The climax of the ritual is the killing of the chicken and the dripping of the blood onto Kent's back. At that moment Salem emerges from the bathroom and asks how Kent is doing. The boy tells her that he is dead, and in fact that they are both dead. Salem does not want to hear that and begins walking in circles, asking to be soothed and comforted.

Resuming the role of son, the boy tells Salem that they will go out to dinner "as soon as daddy's well." Not satisfied, Salem makes a suggestive remark to the boy: "Just look at me. I'm almost naked." On that line the boy begins putting on Kent's costume. While he is doing so, Salem tells him to leave, but by the time he is fully dressed, she is saying, "Look how strong you are. Just look. Now look at me. . . . Come up here with me and let's see what you look like now that you've grown."

With the boy fully in the costume of the hero, Salem begins to lead him around the stage and down into the aisles, offering him for sale to the audience. Salem's treatment of the boy as chattel recalls the boy's story about his brothers and sisters being carried off by Mexican ranchers to work in the fields. More importantly, however, the selling of the boy is presented as being done at the instigation of the father, suggesting that the father is disposing of the son as a potential rival. Near the beginning of her speech, Salem proclaims, "He has come to me from the hills with his father's clothes and his mother's eyes! Look at his hands! How strong! How brave! His father says he is old enough now to work for himself! To work for one of you! To work hard and long! His father has given him over to me for the price of six hogs!"

A boy come to manhood usually leaves the family of his own accord, of course. In this scene, however, the boy is totally passive; he is being expelled from the family, whether that is seen in the psychological terms already suggested or in purely economic terms, as would be the case in a peasant family that could no longer afford to feed all its children. Shepard himself left home at the age of nineteen, and in *The Rock Garden* the boy makes a dramatic and forceful break with the father. At the same time, there runs throughout Shepard's work a longing for the father that is represented in sons talking about fathers and, in a number of cases, of sons taking fathers' places and literally donning their clothes and adopting their mannerisms and attitudes. Shepard's recent family trilogy, *Curse of the Starving Class*, *Buried Child*, and *True West*, expresses these father/son themes in their clearest form.

The contradictory nature of the father/son relationship becomes clear in *La Turista* when Salem's sales pitch is interrupted by a telephone call for the boy. Throughout the brief conversation Salem demands that the boy tell whoever it is that he is going away. When he hangs up, the boy says, "That's my father," to which Salem immediately responds, "Your father is dead," a response which once again suggests the oedipal situation. "You're going with me!" insists Salem, but the boy ignores her and talks about leaving to meet his father. The meeting is projected as a tender one, a reunion recounted in romantic and picaresque cliches, but which ends, as it must, in a parting of the ways.

Unlike most plays, the second act does not continue the action of the first. Instead, it provides a parallel situation in which the ideas of the first act are developed in variation. The set is organized in the same way, but it now represents a hotel room in the States. The bright colors of the Mexican hotel room are replaced by shiny tan and grey, and the telephone and suitcases are plastic. Kent, now wearing long underwear, is sitting in bed asleep with a thermometer in his mouth. Salem is dressed in what Shepard calls "American plastic clothes." A doctor and his son arrive to treat Kent for an illness that causes him to fall asleep frequently. The doctor (Doc) is dressed in Civil War costume and is played by the actor who played the witch doctor in act 1. His son (Sonny) is dressed the same way and is played by the actor who portrayed the boy.

From Salem's description, Kent seems to be suffering from an emotional and psychological condition connected to their relationship or to some deeper alienation in his life. Doc diagnoses Kent's disease in the kind of pseudomedical terms that Kent used to explain sunburn in act 1. The only treatment that Doc can prescribe is to keep Kent in motion, and with Sonny's help Salem begins to walk Kent around the room. In his half-asleep state Kent tells a story about someone coming to his family's house once, a house "in the middle of the prairie, with nothing around but prairie and one huge factory where they make something inside that you never see outside." This bleak American landscape is the setting for an even bleaker family situation in which the father is dying "from lack of everything he needs," as are the sons and daughters also. The visitor then makes the father an offer that is the American-consumer-economy version of the Mexican farmers' raid on the boy's village that was recounted in act 1: "If you change each one of the stupid names you gave your eight kids, from whatever it is now, to one of the eight brand names of our cigarettes, I'll set you up in your own little business and give you all the smokes you need." This offer also recalls the account, in Salem's sales-pitch speech, of the father selling his son for six hogs, while it looks forward to an important action in *Curse of the Starving Class* in which the father sells the family ranch while in a drunken stupor.

Since Kent and Salem are named for cigarettes, this story identifies them as chattel of "the Greatest Society," as people who have been bartered for things. It also suggests that they are brother and sister as well as lovers since the children of the same family have been branded with cigarette names. As such they are examples of the inbreeding that Kent describes in his hero speech in the first act: "Incest! Yes sirree! The land will fall apart." The cleanliness that Kent rails against is in fact sterility, at the heart of which is a deadly social poison, signified in Kent's cigarette speech by the factory from which "all you can see is smoke coming out." Next to this illness, the dysentery from which Kent and Salem suffer is a minor ailment, and, in fact, is even a healthy ailment, since it builds "up a man's immunity to his environment."

"La turista" eventually gives way to a normal condition, but the disease from which Kent suffers in act 2 could result in extinction. As Doc says in his description of the disease, "The illness begins, usually, with rise of temperature and increasing drowsiness or lethargy, which may gradually proceed to a state of complete unconsciousness." An earlier form of this disease appears in *The Rock Garden* in the boy's constant nodding off in boredom. For this simple form of the disease, leaving home may be the cure, but for the more advanced forms there may be nothing that can be done. When Salem tells Doc and Sonny that she is taking Kent to Mexico for rest, Sonny asks, "Why Mexico? Why not Canada, where you'd be less noticeable?" Salem thinks she sees his point and indicates that he is right since in Mexico "they'd notice us right off the bat." Doc, however, adds, "Especially with a corpse," meaning not that Kent is going to die but that in a real sense he is dead already. The boy had said the same thing about both Salem and Kent in act 1. The source of this living death is then emphasized when Sonny says, "They'd notice a corpse anywhere," and Kent responds, "Not here," presumably because that is the common condition in the States.

At this point the father/son motif takes over again but in a few form. Kent begins to question Doc's motives and projects an elaborate image of Doc as a mad scientist who wants to experiment on him. Doc says he only wants to transform "the dying man into a thing of beauty." Kent, however, conjures up the image of a monster, using Frankenstein-like movie scenes to portray the process and results of Doc's "experiments." In Kent's vision Doc becomes father/creator of the monster and then desperately tries to save the monster from the mob of villagers that is chasing him. The two men engage in a verbal duel that inextricably links them. Doc even begins to use the same gestures that Kent used in act 1, and in one of his speeches, he describes himself in the same terms that Salem used to describe the boy when she was offering him for sale. Just as the boy/son took on the role and dress of Kent/father, Doc/father takes on the role and mannerisms of Kent/boy/son. In the final lines of Kent's speech, the distinction between Doc and his monster creation becomes blurred, and they are like one creature. From this complicated give-and-take of father and son, however, Kent escapes. In his role as monster creation, he swings over the heads of Salem, Sonny, and Doc, who, like the mob in Kent's vision, are trying to capture him, and crashes through the wall of the set, leaving only a cutout of his body. But the meaning of the escape is ambiguous since Kent has identified himself with the monster, with a grotesque and mutilated creature who may never be free of his creator, of the father within him.

La Turista marked an important stage in Shepard's career. It demonstrated that he was capable of more sustained work than he had done previously and that he could evaluate and revise what he had written without losing the originality of conception and language that had set him apart in the first place. A present perspective may find faults in the play, but Elizabeth Hardwick was undoubtedly correct about the "impressive literary talent and dramatic inventiveness" of this young author and about *La Turista*'s significance in the development of a new American theater. The play remains today what it was to Hardwick in 1967, "a work of superlative interest."

Two months after *La Turista* opened, the La Mama Experimental Theatre Club staged Shepard's first play to use rock music. He titled it *Melodrama Play* because of its free use of some of the traditional modes of melodrama. As Shepard put it in his original notes for the play, "A production of this play should not be aimed toward making it strictly satirical but more toward discovering how it changes from the mechanism of melodrama to something more sincere."[26] The changes in style of presentation, which Shepard said take place "not just . . . slowly from one thing into the other in the course of the play but rapidly as well and very frequently," are alienating devices, as are the songs which, in a Brechtian way, do "not 'accompany' except in the form of comment."[27]

In characters and situations, *Melodrama Play* looks forward to both *The Tooth of Crime* and *Geography of a Horse Dreamer*. It is about a rock singer and composer, Duke Durgens, who has had one hit song and cannot come up with a second one. His manager, Floyd, gives him until six o'clock to produce, and he sends Duke's brother, Drake, and another musician named Cisco to help him. In the course of a conversation with Duke's girlfriend Dana, Drake claims that he and Cisco actually wrote Duke's hit song. When Floyd returns, he brings a bodyguard, Peter, with him to keep an eye on everybody to make sure they do not leave before they come up with a new song. Peter, however, goes beyond his assignment, and before the play has ended, he has shot Dana and clubbed Duke, Drake, and Cisco.

Ironically, Duke's hit is called "Prisoners, Get Up out of Your Homemade Beds." He himself has become a prisoner of his fame, and all the characters become prisoners of Pe-

26. "Notes on *Melodrama Play*," in *Chicago and Other Plays*, p. 126.
27. "A Short Organum for the Theatre," p. 203.

ter. The song, which is sung in the play by Cisco, urges those immobilized by their own unwillingness or inability to rise to do so before it is too late. Like many of Shepard's plays it ends without any resolution and with two of the characters facing each other in violent confrontation.

Like several of the other plays of this period, *Melodrama Play* acknowledges the existence of the audience. When Duke makes his first appearance, he bows to the audience before he begins singing. A short time later, he sends a letter out into the audience in the form of a paper airplane, and Dana reprimands him: "You ridiculous idiot! You've thrown the letter into the audience. Do you know what that means? That means anyone can pick that letter up and read it!" And in his notes for the play, Shepard indicates that the band should react to the action "like an additional audience." This last element in particular is important since it serves as a device to direct and shape the audience's responses to the stage action.

Although *Melodrama Play* comes early in Shepard's career, it is already a play about the problem of being an artist in a society that consumes art as it does products and that expects the artist to continually surpass himself. When the play opens, Duke is trying to compose a new song but is having trouble. Dana asks him how he is doing, and Duke responds, "Shit. Garbage. Stuff I could have done in school behind everyone's back. Boy. It's terrible. Just terrible. I don't know what to do." Duke's dilemma is emphasized by a university professor who has written to him as part of a research survey. The professor wants to know what changes the hit song has made in his life and what opportunities it has opened up for him. Duke can respond only sarcastically to such a question since the only opportunity that has opened up is the demand to write a new song to sell more records. Duke's manager Floyd makes this quite clear when he tells Duke and Dana, "Right now the thing that bothers us . . . , my colleagues and I, is when will Duke produce for us his next hit tune. When is it that Duke come to us with a shiny new tune that we can sell."

After Floyd leaves, a song played by the band reveals

that the pressure to succeed now confronting Duke has always confronted him, suggesting that it is one of the dominating tensions in American society in general:

> Well ya' grew up small
> Then ya' grew up big
> And the folks in town
> Ask ya' what ya' dig
> And ya' said to them
> Well I hadn't thought
> And they said to you
> Don't let yourself get caught
> Just jerkin' off behind some dark tree
> 'Cause the neighbor's kid got caught doin' that
> And a' course ya' know where he wound up at
> He's now in either
>
> Sing Sing or Alcatraz or either
> Sing Sing or Alcatraz or
> The country zoo
> It's no good for you, boy
> It's no good for you.

The song goes on to tell how he grew to hate people of his hometown who caused the anxiety of accomplishment to develop in him. As a result he hides himself until a man "smokin' behind his desk" offers him a way to success, telling him, "There's a lot a' songs that I got for you." The boy jumps at the chance, only to discover that the man has booked him, for his first date, into either "Sing Sing or Alcatraz or either / Sing Sing or Alcatraz or / The country zoo." For Duke, then, to succeed or not to succeed is not the question since whichever he does will land him in the same place.

To strengthen the song's ability to comment on the action, it is further separated from the body of the work by being loud and fast and by having Duke and Dana do the frug. Also, at the end of the song, Duke and Dana applaud the band, and the band takes a bow. Once again Shepard has taken Brecht as his model: "It emphasizes the general gest of showing, which always underlies that which is being shown, when the audience is musically addressed by means of songs." In order to accomplish this, "the actors ought not to 'drop into' song, but should clearly mark it off from the rest of the text."[28]

On the upstage wall of the set are large black-and-white photographs of Bob Dylan and Robert Goulet. Each represents a different position in the music world, yet they are equal because both pictures are without eyes. When he first appears, Duke is "wearing extra long hair, shades, jeans, boots, vest," clearly linking him to the Bob Dylan photograph. After his third attempt to produce a new song, however, he asks Dana to cut his hair, telling her, "You know I'm stuck and I know it. But I have a surprise for everyone. I have a love song to sing but it has to correspond with the way I look or it just won't work." Failing to be a Dylan musician, he decides to become a Goulet one, a romantic crooner. The change in styles is pointless, of course, since the real problem is not how or what one sings, but singing itself. Like Duke, both Dylan and Goulet are prisoners of their own success and, therefore, are blind models for him to follow.

As Dana is about to cut Duke's hair, Drake and Cisco arrive. Drake immediately begins to taunt Duke: "Nothing going on here, eh! That's funny, Dukie. Every time we come around here there's nothing going on." When Drake learns that Duke wants to cut his hair, he uses it as an opportunity to humiliate and unmask him. Taking the scissors from Dana, Drake gives the haircut himself, at the same time revealing that Duke did not write the song for which he has become famous. Dana at first refuses to believe that Duke stole the song from Drake, but when Duke asks her to buy him a black suit and tie, black shoes, and a white shirt to go along with his new haircut, she realizes that he really did steal the song. In her anger with Duke, she tells Floyd that Duke "stole that song that's made you rich." Floyd responds by ignoring Dana, not because he disbelieves her, but because he does not care. Floyd wants a new song, and if Duke cannot write it, then someone else can.

Floyd's ruthless commercialism is most clearly repre-

28. Ibid., p. 203.

sented in his bringing along a guard to keep an eye on the songwriters to make sure they produce. At one point Duke lunges at Floyd, only to be knocked out by Peter the guard. With Duke out of action, Floyd turns to Drake, who tries to stay out of it by claiming that he is only an accompanist. When Dana gives the lie to this response, Drake then gives his name as Cisco, indicating that the real Cisco, whom he identifies as Drake, is the songwriter. When Dana says they are lying, Floyd characteristically replies, "What difference?" Dana continues to make trouble until Peter shoots her. Duke gains consciousness at this point and sees Dana on the floor. At first, he responds in a manner typical of melodrama: "She's dead. Oh my God." Almost immediately, however, he asks, "Did she get my suit?" This remark not only undercuts the melodrama but also defines the essential opportunism of Duke. It focuses Floyd's attention on Duke as well, making him notice that Duke's hair is short. "What will they say in Phoenix?" demands Floyd. "They won't even know who you are. They'll laugh you right off the stage!"

The play has now reached a second crucial juncture, and to summarize and comment on the action thus far, the band plays another song. This time the music is slower and softer, but once again the actors, with the exception of Dana, dance around the stage. The song seems to address Duke, as did the first one, but this time the condition it describes has a wider application. At the heart of the song is the idea of exploitation and its effect on the artist.

> Who'll open the door
> While you lay on the floor,
> Who'll brush your long hair
> While you just sit and stare
> At the friends all around you
> Who pump you and pound you . . .
> And they just ask you for more
> Of the same that ya' gave
> Of the same that they took.

The climax of the song is an ironic answer to the question it poses: "But don't worry now, whatever you do, / Just do your dance and forget about who."

The song began with the statement "Well now that you're older than ya' was before," which implies the questioning attitude that follows. After giving its ironic answer, however, it makes a new and apparently contradictory statement in its final section: "So that now that you're younger / Than ya' was before." The condition it then describes is completely nonquestioning:

> And ya' can tell that you're younger
> 'Cause ya' don't mind the floor
> Where you crawl up and down
> With your nose to the ground
> And ya' don't mind the smell
> 'Cause you can't even tell
> The difference 'tween heaven and hell any more.

Despite this difference in condition, the song still gives the same advice, though this time the irony is more bitter and more pointed:

> But don't worry now, whatever you do
> Just do your dance and forget about who . . .
> Just eat your food 'cause nobody cares . . .
> And the street doesn't care if ya' just sit and eat
> So eat while ya' can and it all might come true
> 'Cause who is around who can tell what to do
> And who is around who can save you from you,
> Who is around who can save you from you?

When the song is finished, the actors stop dancing, applaud the band, and resume the play. Appropriately, Floyd has the first lines, and he immediately moves the exploitive situation forward. Speaking like a gangster, he orders Drake and Cisco to go to Phoenix in place of Duke. Floyd then leaves, having given Peter instructions to let no one out. Duke, however, tries to talk himself out by telling Peter the whole story of his hit song and by saying that since he is neither Bob Dylan nor Robert Goulet, he has no business being there anymore. Peter seems to give in, but as Duke goes for the door, Peter slugs him. A short time later, he slugs Cisco after telling him he can leave. Only Drake is left conscious, and Peter confronts him with an impossible task: Drake must give "an unbiased opinion" of

Peter's character. To help him, Peter tells Drake a story about encountering a crawling man with no eyes who was trying to get to Arizona. After pointing the man in the right direction, Peter was accosted by a policeman with a club, who forced him into a hallway and made him take off his pants. The story is interrupted by a knock at the door. Some men sent by Floyd have come to take Dana's body, but intent on getting an answer to his question, Peter does not let them in. Peter then takes off his pants, with Drake still insisting that he cannot answer Peter's question. Floyd returns, but Peter will not let him in either. Floyd goes away, and Peter begins hitting Drake with the club, first in the stomach and then on the back. Finally, in desperation, Drake pleads, "Peter, I can't! I'm stuck!"

Peter's story and the actions that follow it call up a number of associations: the man with no eyes parallels the eyeless photographs of Bob Dylan and Robert Goulet; his destination, Arizona, is similar to the site of Duke's next concert, Phoenix; the policeman in Peter's story, with his club and his intimidation of Peter, corresponds to Peter himself; and Drake's final plea to Peter about being stuck for an answer puts Drake in the same position as Duke, who was stuck for a new song. Finally, as the last remaining artist, and perhaps the most genuine one since he actually composed the hit song, Drake is brought down to all fours by Peter's attacks and for the rest of the play crawls around the stage like the eyeless man of the story.

As Drake's pacing becomes more frantic and he begins to hum the new song that Floyd is waiting for, Peter, who has been sitting on the sofa slapping his club into the palm of his hand, turns on the radio. Out comes the voice of Daniel Damon, the sociologist who had written to Duke. His commentary claims that he has just finished interviewing Duke Durgens, but what he says functions as a coda to the play: "So I do hope we have given all of you somewhat of an indication of just exactly how the personal life of an artist is affected and/or altered by the reception of his work by the public at large." Indeed the play has done just that. Exploited, coerced, sold, and sold out, the life of the artist is that of the prisoner of Duke/Drake's hit song:

Well early one night you got so very up tight
And you said this sleepin' it just ain't right
But there was nothin' at all that you could do
'Cause your eyes stayed shut with your homemade
    glue . . .
But when you do awaken from your deep sleep . . .
You'll walk right outside without no name,
You'll walk right outside from where you came.

Despite the dark picture of the artist's predicament that both the action of the play and the song commentaries give, Shepard places the final blame on the artist himself. If the artist is without eyes, the glue that shuts them, as the song makes clear, is homemade, as is the bed in which the artist lies. The solution is to "get up out a' your home-made beds" and be willing to "walk right outside without no name." The attraction to fame is a difficult one for the artist to resist, however, as Shepard indicated in recent comments on his successful and busy acting career: "It's all very tempting. I think you have to find a way to refuse much, much more than you accept, just in order to keep going with your own work."[29]

The rendition of "Prisoners, Get Up out of Your Home-made Beds" that ends the play is incorporated into the general use of songs in the play not only by its content but also by the use of the radio as an alienating device and by the band's joining in with the radio's presentation. Its message is further emphasized when each of the characters who has been lying dead or unconscious on the stage gets up and leaves just before the refrain, "Oh prisoners, won't you get up out a' your homemade beds," is sung. Their response is also the culminating gesture of *Melodrama Play*'s playfulness with the conventions of melodrama and a recognition of the playwright's ability to escape the naive artifice of the conventional theatre.

In November 1967 Shepard's rewrite of his first play, *Cowboys*, was staged at the Mark Taper Forum in Los Angeles. The language of *Cowboys #2* is among the richest in Shepard's early plays; indeed, the play is almost a model

29. Hamill, "The New American Hero," *New York Magazine*, 5 December 1983, p. 102.

for some of Shepard's beliefs about language. "The power of words for me," wrote Shepard, "isn't so much in the delineation of a character's social circumstances as it is in the capacity to evoke visions in the eye of the audience." *Cowboys #2* is, above all else, about this power, about "words as living incantations and not as symbols," about the imagination set free. Perhaps this is just another way of saying that *Cowboys #2* is a play about plays and play-acting since at the heart of the theatrical experience is the language of the text: "Language . . . seems to be the only ingredient . . . that retains the potential of making leaps into the unknown. There's only so much I can do with appearances. Change the costume, add a new character, change the light, bring in objects, shift the set, but language is always hovering right there, ready to move faster and more effectively than all the rest of it put together."[30]

Appropriate to this conception, the play uses a bare stage for its setting, the only prop a sawhorse with a blinking yellow light. When the play opens, the vehicles for the language, Stu and Chet, are seated against the upstage wall on either side of the sawhorse. They are dressed entirely in black. The sawhorse and yellow light suggest an urban environment, but the words speak of the open West. Through what Stu and Chet say, and especially by how they say it, the play evokes worlds of action, changing weather conditions, impressive landscapes, and a period and place in American history that is now the province of myth.

Cowboys #2 begins with an ordinary conversation about rain that could take place anywhere. Almost immediately, however, it is used as a jumping-off point for imaginative play. Stu asks Chet, "Why don't you go over there and see if you can see any cloud formations?" Since there is no stage setting, "over there" can only be another part of the stage and not a specific representation of place, and going "over there" becomes an act of consciousness. To emphasize the imaginative nature of this act, Chet adopts the walk and voice of an old man and addresses Stu as Mel.

30. "Language, Visualization, and the Inner Library," pp. 216–17.

Stu joins right in, also using the voice of an old man and addressing Chet as Clem. After a discussion of the darkness of the clouds, Stu suddenly returns to his normal voice and calls out to Chet, "Hey! Come back!" With this interruption of the imaginative play, Chet again takes his original position upstage.

It then becomes Stu's turn to take on the old man role and to check out the darkness of the clouds. Just before he does, however, a whistling is heard offstage, and both men's attention is drawn to it. The whistling, in the stage directions identified as coming from a character called Man Number Two, seems to act as a catalyst for the renewing of the role-playing. At the end of the play Man Number Two, along with Man Number One, another offstage voice, become onstage characters who quite clearly function in counterpoint to the imaginative activity and language of Stu and Chet.

Throughout the play, Shepard uses sounds to help signify the things and events that Stu and Chet conjure up in their minds. A steady rain is heard, for example, as they role around in imaginary mud. Later, the sounds of horses and screaming Indians accompany a gun battle acted out in the style of the classic Western film. Sounds are also used to contrast the play's dual urban/Western setting: at the beginning the sound of a single cricket, which continues throughout the play, competes with the sound of hammering and sawing; near the end the horse and Indian sounds return and are juxtaposed to car horns. At one point, the car horns are used in concert with Stu's description of suburban sprawl taking over what was once a lush area of orange orchards.

By the end of the play, the distinction between Stu/Chet and Mel/Clem has already disappeared, and the incantatory power of the words has brought about the triumph of the world of imagination. Just before this happens, Stu and Chet deliver monologues in their normal voices, each one setting up a contrast which, in the play's final monologue, gives way to a unified vision.

Stu discourses on what Shepard would later call the "true West," meaning by that term both the West as it is today, landscapes of houses and shopping centers, and the West as it once was, an open and natural environment. Speaking of the orange groves that once covered the area, Stu laments, "They were all over. Then they cut them down, one at a time. Every one. Built schools for kids and homes for old flabby ladies and halls for heroes and streets for cars and houses for people." As he continues, animal metaphors take over to describe, in graphic terms, a civilization dying in its own wastes: "peacocks shitting in people's driveways"; pet turtles dying in their pans of water, until "the whole house starts smelling from dead turtles and rotten stems and slimy water"; and infected chickens that "lie there in a pool of shit and pus and feathers and cluck."

Throughout this apocalyptic vision, car horns are sounding from offstage, and both Stu and Chet look at the audience, as if they are looking at the scene Stu describes. At the end of the monologue, Stu withdraws to an upstage position and lies down, soon to become totally inert. Chet, however, responds almost comically. After a long pause, he quite casually remarks, "It's a nice morning though," and then launches into a monologue about different kinds of food he likes. To his description of food is contrasted a conversation from offstage between Man Number One and Man Number Two. Sounding probably like the young Sam Shepard and Charlie Mingus or the fictional Stu and Chet in their East Village apartment, they discuss how their rent has been cut to one dollar a month because of some ruling of "the City Health Department or Rent Commission." Like the other offstage sounds, this conversation presents an urban reality that contrasts sharply with Stu's and Chet's imaginative outpourings.

After a brief transition in which Chet talks about how bad their bodies and clothes smell, the old western landscape takes over. Chet switches back to his old-man voice and describes the heat of the desert and how they must find water if they are to survive. With it still morning and the temperature already ninety degrees, Chet/Clem speculates that it could go as high as a hundred and twenty. "We got to find some shade," he tells Mel. Not getting any

60

response, he returns to his normal voice: "Okay, Stu, this isn't funny. I don't think it's funny. You're going to sleep all day while I bust my ass looking for shade?" Stu still does not respond. Rather than abandon the desert scene, however, Chet drags Stu's body downstage where "there's better shade." Dipping his hat into a stream and pouring water over Stu's face, Chet once again takes on the old-man voice. He describes his tongue cracking from the heat and the vultures circling overhead. Taking off his shirt and vest, he covers Mel's head to protect him from the scorching sun.

In the final moments, Man Number One and Man Number Two enter. They are the same age as Chet and Stu, though they are dressed more conventionally in suits. With scripts in hand, they begin reading the play. Their dry reading contrasts markedly with the living image being projected by Chet, who has carried the audience fully into the world of two old desert rats dying from the heat and waiting to be prey for the vultures. Yet the reading of the play is crucial, for it reveals the text behind the speeches and brings the author out from under cover, thus revealing something of the illusion that is at work on the audience. From the words emerges a myth, a "sense of mystery" that does not "speak only to the mind and leave out completely the body" but that speaks to both equally. "I see an old man by a broken car in the middle of nowhere," wrote Shepard, "and those simple elements right away set up associations and yearnings to pursue what he's doing there." In *Cowboys #2*, as in many of his other plays, Shepard does not make this pursuit alone; he takes the audience with him.[31]

Before 1967 ended, a fourth Shepard play, *Forensic and the Navigators*, reached the public. It was presented by Theatre Genesis under the direction of Ralph Cook and featured O-Lan Johnson, whom Shepard later married, in one of the lead roles. Apparently fueled by the antiwar movement of the sixties, it was Shepard's most directly political play up to that point, though its politics are at best fuzzy.

31. Ibid., p. 217.

Perhaps, it is more accurate to say that the play is less about politics than about the political feeling of the time, the confused conflicts between a frightened authority and the diverse and often unfocused "armies of the night" that challenged it. Ten years later, Shepard looked back on this period of "shattered feeling" and proclaimed, "I don't want to get back to the sixties! The sixties sucked dogs! The sixties never happened!"[32]

The title of the play itself suggests an ironic attitude toward the political turmoil of the time. *Forensic* is a form of argumentative debate, more an exercise than a practical application. Its use as a character name calls into question the seriousness of the revolutionary activity of the main characters, both of whom, in the course of the play, are referred to as Forensic. In addition, one of the antagonists, 1st Exterminator, is also called by this name. The second term in the title, *Navigators*, indicates the charting of a course, yet the planning of the revolutionary characters never leads to action; in fact, they spend most of their time hiding. Further, the linking of a single name *Forensic* with the more general *Navigators* makes the joint designation, *Forensic and the Navigators*, sound like a sixties rock group.

The play begins with Forensic and his co-conspirator Emmet debating strategy. A plan to storm a desert fortress where political prisoners are being kept has just been abandoned. Emmet explains why it would be impossible to accomplish, while Forensic argues for some kind of action. They have nearly come to blows when Oolan enters carrying a frying pan with one pancake in it. The boys, in a characteristically bourgeois way, have been waiting for Oolan to bring their breakfast. Walking around the table and flipping the pancake in the pan, she sarcastically remarks on how uptight they get if they do not get fed on time. She flips the pancake onto the table, causing Emmet to complain, "How many times I gotta tell you I don't eat that buckwheat Aunt Jemima middle-class bullshit. I want Rice Krispies and nothing else." The contradiction in Emmet's statement is clear, leading Forensic to accuse him,

32. *Rolling Thunder Logbook*, p. 135.

"Emmet, you're as soft and flabby as you say your enemies are." Faced with these two middle-class kids playing at revolution, one of whom is dressed as a cowboy and the other as an Indian, Oolan has no choice but to be sarcastic.

Suddenly, the Exterminators knock at the door and demand entrance. They are dressed like California Highway Patrolmen and have orders to exterminate the place from top to bottom. Forensic and Emmet manage to temporarily throw them off the track by moving the table and causing the Exterminators to become unsure if they are in the right house. One of the Exterminators leaves to call the home office while the other stays and begins kissing and caressing Oolan, who has fainted. While he is doing this, Forensic and Emmet take his equipment, including his gun. With the 1st Exterminator their prisoner, Emmet decides that the authorities must be on to them and that they "temporarily have to abandon the idea of temporarily abandoning the project and throw ourselves once again into the meat of the game." He also orders Oolan to get him the Rice Krispies.

While Oolan is out of the room, Forensic suggests trading her for information about the fortress. Since the 1st Exterminator has fallen in love with her (he has already pictured them going off together and living in a tree house like Tarzan and Jane), he agrees to Forensic's plan. As Forensic interrogates him, Emmet ravenously devours bowls of Rice Krispies, which Oolan keeps replenishing. At the height of the interrogation, the 2nd Exterminator returns. Emmet and Forensic rush around not knowing what to do, until Forensic tells Oolan to get under the table. As she does so, the 1st Exterminator joins her and Emmet yells, "Take the Krispies!" The Rice Krispies now safe under the table, Emmet and Forensic wrestle for possession of the gun and argue over how to answer the 2nd Exterminator, who demands to be let in. After breaking down the door, the 2nd Exterminator warns them to leave because others are coming to gas the place. He also claims to have "quit the whole business" himself and speculates that his partner has done the same thing. When he discovers that the 1st Exterminator is under the table, he engages him in a conversation that duplicates the one that Forensic and Emmet had at the beginning of the play. Finally, he declares that he will never go "out there . . . again." During the final moments a blue smoke begins to invade the stage, and it continues to spread until it pours over the audience as well. When the smoke clears, the stage is empty; actors, props, and furniture have all disappeared.

The end of *Forensic and the Navigators* recalls both the formal strategy of *Fourteen Hundred Thousand*, in which the play reveals its own theatrical nature, and the images of apocalypse and extinction found in *Chicago* and *Icarus's Mother*. It also reveals the dual influence of Samuel Beckett, in the absurdity of its humor and the impotence of its protagonists, and Bertolt Brecht, in its use of reflexive staging techniques. Three years later Shepard would again deal with the problem of political action in *Operation Sidewinder*, though in much more defined terms and within a structure of far greater formal and cultural complexity. Both plays, however, reveal a skepticism of radical dissent and political solutions. In Shepard, discontents and the desire to do something about them are approached more from a personal than a social perspective and are treated as psychological rather than political questions. Like a mythical cowboy hero, Shepard seems to opt for individual action and a willingness, if not a necessity, to go it alone.

The haze of blue smoke that swept the characters and set of *Forensic and the Navigators* from the stage took Sam Shepard also. Despite the prolific outpouring of plays in 1967 and the significant recognition that followed for Shepard, including Obie awards for *La Turista*, *Melodrama Play*, and *Forensic and the Navigators* and grants from the Rockefeller and Guggenheim foundations, no new Shepard play appeared for almost the next two years. Instead, his energies were directed toward the screen. He was contracted to write the script for Italian director Michelangelo Antonioni's second English-language film, *Zabriskie Point*. Although Shepard's script was discarded in favor of a more political one, the association with Antonioni must have been essentially positive since Shepard later included the director's name among those who provided "keen inspiration" for *Operation Sidewinder*. On a less glamorous scale, Shepard also co-authored the script for Robert Frank's 1968 film *Me and My Brother*. Today, Shepard's involvement with the cinema has brought him to the threshold of stardom as an actor, but in the late sixties it was only an interlude on the road to becoming one of America's most important playwrights.

When Shepard returned to the stage in 1969, it was with one of his most autobiographical plays, *The Holy Ghostly*. It was produced by the La Mama New Troupe and was directed by Tom O'Horgon for a tour of European and American colleges and universities. If *The Rock Garden* is, as Shepard has said, about leaving his family, then *The Holy Ghostly* is a close look at some of the feelings behind that leaving, especially as they relate to his father.

The action is set in the desert, which from this point on in Shepard's plays will be often associated with the father. Particularly prominent is the never-seen father of the estranged brothers of *True West*, who is at the center of many of their conversations. Like this absent character, and for similar reasons, Shepard's own father lived the life of a recluse. "My Dad lives alone on the desert," he wrote in 1979. "He says he doesn't fit with people."[33] Pop in *The Holy Ghostly* is clearly modeled on the real Samuel Shepard Rogers, just as Pop's son, Ice, is a figure for the author himself.

When the play opens, Ice is squatting next to a campfire roasting marshmallows, and Pop is sleeping. Ice sings softly about a young man who has been rambling "'round the town." Later we learn that Ice, like Shepard after leaving home, has moved to New York, a place that Pop disapproves of. Ice has come to help his father deal with the Chindi, a ghost that is out to kill him, but from the beginning, it is evident that the relationship between father and son is not a good one. Pop adopts an authoritarian tone with Ice, as if his son is still a little boy, and he puts down whatever it is that Ice is trying to accomplish in New York. Nevertheless, Pop and Ice are inextricably linked; Pop feels

33. *Motel Chronicles*, p. 56.

that Ice is the only one he can rely on to help him, and Ice, though reacting negatively to Pop, declares himself the "spittin' image of his old man." Further emphasizing a kind of father/son identity, Ice claims, "Why if it weren't for the age separatin' 'em you'd think they was the same person."

The Chindi, however, is the principal device that links father and son. In describing it, Pop says that it has "more arms and legs than the two of us put together," a remark that is meant to identify the Chindi with both of them. Ice suggests a similar thing when he proposes a strategy for scaring the Chindi away: "If we split up, one of us behind, me behind and you in front. We'd get him in the middle." Situating the ghost between father and son in this way implies that it can be seen as some kind of mediating and shared influence, and it is in fact developed in this way as the play progresses. Early in the play, the Chindi is also identified with Pop—"You told me he looked just like you," says Ice—and later with Ice himself, when Pop thinks the Chindi is just Ice in disguise. Before the actual appearance of the Chindi, a witch confronts Pop with the accusation that he himself is a ghost and therefore should go with the Chindi peacefully.

Having implied that the Chindi is really within Pop, the witch goes on to explain that a ghost is "one who has died without finishing what he had to do on the earth . . . because they never found out what they were here for. . . . A ghost is hung up between being dead and being alive because he doesn't know where he's at. We're here to show you exactly where you're at." The "we" in this last sentence also includes Ice, who tells Pop that he has talked with the Chindi: "You know what he told me? He told me that you were dead and you don't even know it." Like the Holy Ghost of the New Testament that descended on the disciples on the day of Pentecost, the Chindi endows Ice with knowledge and the ability to speak in tongues. He responds to Pop in a language that Pop will understand. Until now Ice had attempted to pacify Pop, but with his new knowledge, he begins to curse him. He calls him a "pathetic creep" and voices years of resentment for the way in which Pop had used him as a slave and forced him to listen to his "bullshit about 'improve your mind, you'll never get ahead, learn how to lose, hard work and guts and never say die.'" Finally, he tells Pop that he is going to kill him "once and fer all."

Before this ultimate confrontation comes, Ice and Pop switch roles. Pop begins talking like a little boy and curls up in Ice's lap to hear a story. Ice tells him about a super sun and a giant ice planet that collided, only to explode when the steam generated by the melting ice accumulated to an insupportable point. From the fragments of the explosion was born the solar system, all parts of which became covered with ice except the earth. "Ever since then," concludes Ice, "the earth has been carrying on a constant struggle between fire and ice." Changing out of his little boy role, Pop labels the story "bull pukey," though his next comment implies that on the metaphoric level the story is true: "I'll tell ya' who's gonna make and break this planet, boy. We are! You and me and nothing else!" If it was not clear from the story itself, it is clear now that the struggle between fire and ice is the struggle between father and son. Ice then carries out his threat and shoots Pop in the stomach. Although Pop initially staggers around the stage holding his stomach, he soon discovers that he is not hurt because Ice was right about his being a corpse. As the play ends, the entire theater is consumed in the flames of the campfire, with Pop dancing in them shouting "Burn, Burn" over and over again.

The most direct biographical references come in a monologue that Pop delivers after Ice has gone off looking for the Chindi. Speaking as if to Ice, he describes their past relationship as being more like brothers than like father and son. This view contrasts sharply with the one that Ice gives later when he denounces Pop as a creep. From Pop's perspective Ice has deliberately tried to hurt him. "Right from the start I knowed that," laments Pop. "Like the way ya' changed yer name and all. That was rotten, Stanley. I give ya' that name 'cause that was my name and my Pappy gave me that name and his Pappy before him. That name was handed down for seven generations, boy." Shepard has described how he also changed his name and cut off a patrimony that had gone on for seven generations. The degree to which Shepard's own action should be seen as a rejection of his father is not clear, but in *The Holy Ghostly* the change from the name Stanley Hewitt Moss the seventh to the obviously significant Ice is clearly meant to signify a deep-rooted antagonism. At the end of this monologue, Ice returns wearing Indian war paint and carrying a drum, a get-up that contrasts with Pop's description of his son as having "my eyes and my nose and my mouth . . . my own flesh and blood," and links Ice with the Chindi, whom Pop sees as trying to kill him.

Throughout this conflict between father and son, there is the underlying image of the cowboy and the sense of violence that is associated with the old West. Gunplay abounds in *The Holy Ghostly*, from the first moment that Pop awakes, pulls a gun from under his pillow, and aims at Ice until his attempt to kill the Chindi with a bazooka. Ice even dresses as a cowboy, though an Eastern version of one, and Pop often adopts the accent of a western dirt farmer. Also implied is the image of the old gunfighter who must be on guard against the youngster who may be faster on the draw and who wants to take his place. Immediately after the speech in which Ice finally expresses his resentment for the past, he orders Pop to go for his gun. Pop tries to talk him out of a gunfight, but Ice only responds with, "Draw, old timer."

This classic confrontation is, of course, another variation on the father/son theme, a theme which becomes progressively more important in subsequent Shepard plays. Pop spells out this fear of being replaced quite specifically in yet another form: "I suppose ya' thought I'd drop over dead out a' sheer fright. . . . Then with yer old man out a' the way you could step right in and take over the ranch, lock, stock and barrel. All six hundred acres and the sheep to boot." Since there is no indication that Pop, in fact, owns a ranch any longer, his speech is purely the stuff that movies are made of and is meant to invoke this conventional situation as a sign for the elemental conflict between father and son that is at the heart of the play. In dealing with this theme, *The Holy Ghostly* transcends its apparent autobiographical and specific elements and, more than any of the previous plays, rises to the level of the universal and the general. As a result, the relationship between Pop and Ice, which refers to Shepard and his own father, also signifies all those fathers and sons in the history of Western literature who have struggled with the ties that both bind and separate.

As the decade drew to a close, the La Mama Experimental Theatre Club staged a new Shepard play that brought together a number of the elements he had been working with over the past five years. *The Unseen Hand* is a science-fantasy western parable about freedom, partly intended as a response to the constrictions of the political environment in the late 1960s and to the growing pressures of Shepard's artistic success. As such it strongly recalls *Melodrama Play* and *Forensic and the Navigators*, though it goes beyond both in its description of the problems and in its suggestion of a solution.

As the play begins, the audience is confronted with a stage littered with the refuse of contemporary American society. A battered '51 Chevy convertible sits abandoned center stage, tires gone, top in shreds, a relic of pre-interstate roads. Written across its side in red paint are the words "Kill Azusa," the calling card of rival Arcadia High teenagers. All over are tin cans, boxes, Coke bottles, and the assorted junk of a disposable economy. The sound and lights of a passing diesel truck invade the darkness and fade away, only to recur throughout the play. Together these elements present a striking metaphor for American culture at the end of the sixties, a discarded past surrounded by the no deposit, no return artifacts of the present, with the transport to the future speeding by in the night.

Out of the backseat of the Chevy climbs Blue Morphan, dressed in jeans and cowboy boots but wearing an overcoat. Blue is also a relic of the past, a 120-year-old western desperado who has been living in the Chevy for twenty years and in his memories for even longer. With his two brothers, Cisco and Sycamore, who were gunned down in

1886, he was on his way to becoming a famous outlaw and might have made it into the history books had it not "been fer the old hooch." His first name indicates his long term addiction, *blue* being a slang term for drunk in the mid-nineteenth century, while his last name suggests both Morpheus, the Greek god of dreams, and the drug morphine. In his slightly drunken state, he delivers a long monologue in which he thanks an imaginary driver of the car for giving him a lift, warning him against picking up "longhairs" and inviting him to drop by if he ever passes through Duarte. He also contrasts the past, in which "a Man would have hisself a misunderstanding and go out and settle it with a six gun," with the present, in which everything is "silent, secret . . . when they'll cut ya' down and . . . ya' don't know who done it."

Into this world of hidden forces comes Willie, the space freak, dressed futuristically in "orange tights, pointed shoes, a vinyl vest with a black shirt." His skin is burned and covered with red sores, and on the top of his shaved head is a black hand print. Willie has traveled through two galaxies to enlist the Morphan brothers' help in a battle to free his home planet, Nogoland, from control of the Sorcerers of the High Commission. In a description that both parallels and parodies the process of evolution, Willie tells Blue how he is descended from a race of "fierce baboons that were forced into human form by the magic of the Nogo," a word that puns on the Greek and Christian uses of the term *Logos*, the controlling principle or divine word that is the primal creative force in the universe. Having evolved beyond the capacities of their controllers, they have been put under the domination of the Unseen Hand. "Whenever our thoughts transcend those of the magicians," explains Willie, "the Hand squeezes down and forces our minds to contract into non-preoccupation." Should they try to escape, they are punished by pain and nightmarish visions.

Blue's reponse to this explanation is from the perspective of having lived beyond his time: "What do ya' want me to do about all this? I'm just a juicer on the way out." The answer, beyond the obvious pun involving Blue's name, which hints that relief can be found in morphine, is in Blue and his brothers being part of another world that the rulers of Nogoland cannot understand. The High Commissioners exist in an entirely intellectual state while the Morphans are men of action, physical beings. "If you came into No-goland blazing your six guns they wouldn't have any idea how to deal with you. . . . You would be too real for their experience," explains Willie. The reasoning behind this plan is similar to the distinction that Blue made between the out-front dealings of the past and the "silent, secret" ones of the present. Willie refers to the rulers of the High Commission as the Silent Ones, and so associates them with the forces described by Blue.

Soon after Willie tells his story, he goes into a spasm induced by the Unseen Hand that sends him rolling and screaming on the ground and finally renders him uncon-scious. At this point Cisco Morphan enters, having been called up from the grave by Willie. Once over his surprise at seeing Cisco, Blue tells him about the modern world: cars, radio stations on the moon, spaceships, the Highway Patrol, can openers. Cisco says that their brother Sycamore should be along soon too. Before he arrives, however, a drunken male cheerleader wearing an Azusa High School sweater comes on, screaming back at some rival Arcadia kids who have beaten him. On first seeing Cisco in his western clothes, the Kid calls him a "hippie creep" and then a "commie faggot." Cisco finally quiets him down by drawing his gun, and the Kid breaks down and begs to be allowed to stay there because he is afraid to go home. In an apparent rejection of football and cheerleading, he vows never to cheer again.

Willie regains consciousness and implements the next stage of his plan: he makes Blue young again, though in the middle of the procedure the Hand takes control of him and he goes into another spasm. Cisco and Blue celebrate resurrection and youth by doing somersaults, singing "Rock Around the Clock," and doing the twist. At last Syc-amore shows up. He is dressed like the legendary western figure Bat Masterson, and immediately he begins to ques-tion the whole plan that has brought them together. In fact, he tries to talk them out of going to Nogoland so that they can return to their own business as robbers. When he finds out that there are no longer any trains to rob, he decides that they might as well go after all.

Willie, who has since awakened, outlines the terrain of his planet. While he is doing this, Sycamore drags on the Kid, who has been listening in on Willie's description. The kid justifies himself by telling them he can help them, and then proceeds to deliver a lecture on revolution and guer-rilla warfare. This turns out to be a ruse, and the Kid grabs Sycamore's gun and says he is going to turn them in as subversives because they are planning to take over Azusa. Although this action represents a misunderstanding of Willie's plan, it does suggest a link between Nogoland and Azusa, and since Azusa has several times been identified by the slogan "Everything from A to Z in the USA," the link is extended to the United States as a whole. The Kid may have misunderstood Willie, but he has heard Shepard loud and clear.

The Kid then launches into a speech that enumerates all the things he loves about Azusa. The list is a compendium of the stock items of middle-class American life in the fifties and early sixties, including drive-in movies, bowling alleys, liquor stores, the high school, the Bank of America, the sock hop, white bucks, madras shorts, and mom. At the conclusion of this affirmation, Willie goes into a trance and begins speaking in an unknown language that endows him with great power. The Kid fires repeatedly at Willie but without effect. Finally, the Kid clutches his head and falls to the ground screaming; Willie has discovered the secret of the High Commission. The Hand is now under his control, and he realizes that his people are free. "It was all in my brain the whole time," exclaims Willie. "The an-cient language of the Nogo. Right in my brain. . . . They have no control. We can do what we want! We're free to do what we want." Since Willie has the power, Cisco asks him to call back all the old gang from the past, but Willie tells him that he too has the power and that he can do it himself. The Unseen Hand is a creation of their own minds; they are their own jailers and their own liberators.

Having discovered this truth, Willie leaves to return home. Blue, Cisco, and Sycamore do not seem to have gotten the message, however, and they question what they, as men out of their time, should do next in this hostile environment of Azusa. Cisco suggests, "We could change our names. Get a haircut, some new threads. Blend right in." Sycamore agrees: "I could get me an office job easy enough. . . . Get me a car maybe." But Blue meanwhile has decided to leave: "I been hangin' around this dump fer twenty years. Seems about time to get the lead out. . . . Right now I just gotta move. That's all I know."

Blue and Cisco leave, not with an idea of what they can do or where they can go, but at least with the knowledge that it is "time to get the lead out." After twenty years, Blue recognizes that he is free to move, and the audience, if it believes Willie, understands that he was always free to move. Sycamore, on the other hand, opts to stay, and as a result immediately begins to grow older. In an "ancient voice" he talks to the imaginary driver of the '51 Chevy, just as Blue did at the beginning of the play. He climbs into the back seat of the car and is lost to sight, leaving the audience with the self-justification that he has "to take stock a' things."

A poem that Shepard wrote in 1980 deals quite directly with this kind of self-imposed inactivity, especially as it is used by artists to explain their inability to produce.

Now lemme get this straight

You say
You're tortured because you can't write
Or
You can't write because you're tortured

You say
These times have made you cynical
Or
These times confirm your cynicism

Now lemme say one thing . . .

Your despair is more boring
Than *The Merv Griffin Show* . . .

73

Get off your tail and cook
Do time
Anything
But don't burn mine[34]

For Shepard, the artist should be a man of action, the desperado of the intellectual world whose work is like blazing six guns, and if it is not, he has no one to blame but himself. Whatever prisons he is in are of his devising; the handprint on his head is his own.

If the message of *The Unseen Hand* was good enough for the artist, then perhaps it was good enough for the country. During a period when the government was at war with many of its own people and when the forces of change were often in disarray and retreat, Willie's parting advice to the Morphan brothers, "This is your world. Do what you want with it," had a wider political application. It implied that the power of the oppressor or of the system was not so much a power that had been taken as a power that had been given by the very people it oppressed, in much the same way that the pressures toward conventionality and commercialism put on art needed the acquiescence of the artist in order to succeed.

The sixties had brought major changes in the life of Sam Shepard. At the beginning of the decade, he was an unknown teenager living in Duarte, California, and was potentially headed for a career as a veterinarian. Almost by accident, however, he found himself becoming an actor in a small traveling theater company, though it may have been the traveling more than the acting that had moved him in this direction. Somewhere in these years, Shepard also developed an aspiration to write, and by 1964 he had put this aspiration to work in the theater. With the production of his first plays, *Cowboys* and *The Rock Garden*, Shepard's future was determined, despite the generally poor reception the plays received. Time has proved the one positive review, Michael Smith's enthusiastic praise in the *Village Voice*, to have been correct. Not only did it save the plays, but it encouraged Shepard to continue writing. By

34. Ibid., p. 54.

the end of the decade, in the short span of six years, sixteen of his plays had been staged, and Sam Shepard had become an important voice in an emerging new American theater. In addition, he had written a screenplay for one of the world's great film directors, had been awarded an Obie for distinguished plays, and had been recognized with grants from both the Rockefeller and Guggenheim foundations. He was twenty-six years old and on the threshold of national prominence. What he would achieve in the coming decade, primarily through an extraordinary command of language, would place him among America's great writers.

III. Playing for High Stakes

When an interviewer suggested that more careful craftsmanship had gone into the writing of *The Tooth of Crime* than into the earlier plays, Sam Shepard responded that the difference was not in the size of the play but in the stakes for which he was playing. "You can play for the high stakes or the low stakes," he added; ". . . what makes a play is how true it is to the stakes that you defined at the beginning."[1] By the end of the sixties Shepard had already begun playing for higher stakes, but as the new decade opened, they were raised even more with the most complex and ambitious of his plays to date, *Operation Sidewinder*. Coincidentally, and essentially unrelated to Shepard's sense of higher stakes, this play marked the official recognition of its author's important place in the modern American theatre. It was commissioned by the prestigious Vivian Beaumont Theatre at New York's Lincoln Center.

Summarizing some of the personal and cultural influences that fed into *Operation Sidewinder*, Shepard dedicated it to Michelangelo Antonioni, Crazy Horse, the Rolling Stones, the Holy Modal Rounders (who provided the music for the play), the Hopi Indians, Gabby Hayes, Old Oraibi (one of the original Hopi settlements), Mickey Free (a half-breed Indian associated with the legend of Geronimo), 1968, and his wife O-Lan. Particularly important to the action of the play are the political events of the late sixties, most pointedly represented in the year 1968, and the rituals and religious beliefs of the Hopi. Out of these two contrasting cultural contexts, Shepard fashions a response to the time that suggests there is a greater need for spiritual renewal than for political action. That is not to say that Shepard does not see a need for change—in fact, the play sharply criticizes the established political system—but rather that the need arises out of a lack of meaningful,

1. Chubb, "Metaphors," p. 199.

humane cultural values, which themselves cannot be restored by the immediate concerns of a narrow ideology.

At the heart of *Operation Sidewinder* is a large rattlesnake, which functions structurally as both the principal causal agent and the link between the play's conflicting political and metaphysical forces. When the play opens, the sidewinder is seen undulating mechanically, bathed in a yellow light that seems to emanate from itself. The sound of a jet loudly breaks the desert quiet, punctuated only by the snake's rattling and the distant howl of a coyote. A car screeches to a halt, and out get a man and a woman to photograph the giant snake. Without warning, the sidewinder lunges at the woman, identified as Honey by the man, and wraps itself tightly around her. The man tells his wife to relax and runs off to find a forest ranger to help them. The lights black out, and scene 1 is brought to an end by a song entitled "Do It Girl." As he had done earlier in *Melodrama Play*, Shepard uses the songs to comment on the action in a Brechtian manner. In this case, the song's sexual content endows the snake with phallic connotations that become quite specific in scene 3 when Honey has an orgasm in response to the sidewinder's undulations.

With scene 1 the basic episodic structure of the play is established. Act 1 contains eight disjunctive scenes and act 2 has four; at the end of each scene, with the exception of the last one in act 2, which uses Hopi chants throughout, a song is used as a separate element to outline and comment on the scene's content.

Scene 2 switches to a desert garage where a hippie-looking young man is having his Volkswagen fixed. As the mechanic works, the young man becomes more and more impatient. When Honey's husband, Duke, runs in seeking help, the young man can no longer contain his impatience and shoots both Duke and the mechanic. The young man flees, and "Pipeline," a song about confusion, going around in circles, and the need to find a way out, is heard in the dark.

Scene 3 returns to Honey and the sidewinder and introduces the character Billy, an old prospector modeled on Gabby Hayes. He is crouched down next to Honey giving her a history of mining in the area when the young man enters and gives Billy a gun, which is to be passed on to Mickey Free. Both leave, caring not at all about Honey's predicament. During the blackout "Generalonely" is played, a song about being lonely and blue that puns with word combinations such as general only, generally lonely, lonely general, and only a general.

Scene 4 reveals the vital information that the sidewinder is really an Air Force computer that has escaped. It is capped off with the ironic drug song "Catch Me," which taunts, "Catch me if you can while I last 'cause there's nothing' to keep me around."

The end of "Catch Me" blends into the rattle of the sidewinder that begins the next scene. Honey is still held firmly by the snake, and Mickey Free and two other Indians are watching her. All three are dressed in Apache costume of the late 1800s, as befits the origin of the Mickey Free character. In response to her plea for help, Mickey Free cuts off the head of the sidewinder and drops it into a pouch that he wears around his waist. Honey casts off the body of the snake and collapses. The young man arrives and gives Mickey two bags of dope, which he is to put into the Air Force water supply. Mickey reveals that he is doing this in order to rid the sky of the "silver birds" and so please the Spider Woman. The Indians leave, and the young man proceeds to give himself a fix, telling Honey he is a diabetic. Feeling her energy depleted from the ordeal with the snake, she naively asks for an injection in order to raise her sugar level. The young man gives her one, and the scene ends with a comic drug song entitled "Euphoria."

The setting for scene 6 is a fast-food drive-in where three black revolutionaries discuss the plan to drug the Air Force water. The leader, Blood, explains how the drug will cause the pilots to fly to "a little island just south of Miami," while another questions whether the young man is reliable enough to carry out his part. The carhop who took their order comes on with a speech about revolutionary brotherhood, which the three blacks ignore, sarcastically referring to her as S.D.S.

The fantastic nature of the drugging plan—one of the blacks even compares it to James Bond—is topped only by the carhop's condescending belief in what she calls the "whole unity thing that you guys are into" and the casual way in which she uses the language of armed struggle. The blacks' plan is reminiscent of the Yippies' mocking threat at the 1968 Democratic Convention in Chicago to put LSD into the city water supply. The difference, of course, is that for the Yippies the threat was a form of street theater played out under the insatiable and often gullible eye of the mass media while the three revolutionaries in Shepard's play discuss their plan in all seriousness. As for the white carhop's verbal flirtation with revolution and her attempt to identify with the oppression suffered by black people, its level of reality is probably best summarized in her statement, "I mean you people have such a groovy thing going," to which Blood responds laconically, "Yeah, right." The satiric quality of this scene is then stressed by the concluding song, which puts the whole thing in a broader context by relating it ironically to the popular sixties concept of synergy and to the flower child mentality of some of the protest movement:

> Come along, sing with me a song of synergy
> Find that peace in your soul
> We're all one and heaven is our goal
> Synergy will get us all and it's going to be a ball
> Kick that gong, ring that bell, synergy will save us all from hell . . .
> Get undressed, plant a tree, make love to machinery
> Throw away all the locks, open up the jails and stop the clocks
> We can have paradise right now at a bargain price.

Having given the antiestablishment forces a satiric treatment, Shepard then does the same for the establishment. In scene 7 the Air Force scientist, Dr. Vector, a take-off on Dr. Strangelove, describes the nature and function of the sidewinder computer, which, contrary to instructions, he has set free on the desert so that it could accumulate knowledge and reach the "realm of extraterrestrial consciousness" through communication with beings from other planets. Dr. Vector's joy at this prospect contrasts sharply with the fact that Mickey Free has already cut the head off this two-billion-dollar experiment. Even more ironically, Mickey will use the sidewinder in a Hopi ritual that will achieve a more genuine form of higher consciousness than that proposed by Dr. Vector. The failure of Dr. Vector's plan and the hopeless condition of the sidewinder are then expressed in the song "Dusty Fustchens," which ends the scene: "Don't leave me dying in the desert / Don't leave me dangling in the dust / I don't wanna live here with these here lizards / They look at me with a cold and hungry lust."

Act 1 concludes with a scene between Honey and the young man in which he expresses his feelings of alienation and rails against Nixon, Wallace, Humphrey, and the political system that is killing soldiers and blacks. He talks of taking over the Democratic party in four years, but until then he feels "depressed, deranged, decapitated, dehumanized, defoliated, demented and damned." While the young man is speaking, the body of the sidewinder begins to move in response to flashing blue lights in the sky. Finally, the young man launches into a wild metaphoric speech about being an American. It is filled with contradictions and a tremendous sense of alienation; in its confusions it is a precise expression of the feelings of many young people in the sixties: "I am from Freak City. . . . A town like any other town. A town like Mama used to make with lace doilies and apple pie and incest and graft. No. It's not true. I am an American though. Despite what they say. In spite of the scandal. I am truly an American. I was made in America. . . . I devour the planet. I'm an earth eater. No. I'm a lover of peace. A peace maker. A flower child, burned by the times." The scene blacks out, and an intermission sign begins blinking on and off as the Holy Modal Rounders sing "Alien Song," which describes the feelings of alienation that a young man experiences returning to his childhood home and discovering that "it doesn't seem like I was ever here."

As act 2 begins, the young man and Honey are prisoners of the three black revolutionaries, who have learned that

Mickey Free has double-crossed them by not putting the dope in the Air Force water supply but instead by taking off into the desert with the sidewinder computer. The young man protests that he knows nothing about this, but Blood holds him responsible, sending Honey and him off to find Mickey and to bring back the sidewinder. It is also revealed that the young man has killed Duke and the garage mechanic, an act that Blood considers to be stupid, although he himself kills a forest ranger before the scene ends. The young man's attempt to justify his failures is treated satirically in the song "Bad Karma," which includes the refrain "I try so hard / I try to behave / But that bad karma baby gonna lead me to my grave."

With the second scene, the play begins moving in a new direction. The political machinations of act 1 come into direct conflict with the religious mysticism of act 2. Mickey is with an "old Indian shaman," the Spider Lady, and in his lap is the head of the sidewinder. The Spider Lady tells Mickey about an imminent war that will end the Fourth World and usher in the Fifth and about a spiritual conflict with material things. She also tells him the myth of the Lizard and Snake Clans, how a battle over a great spirit snake caused the snake to be torn in two, "the head going to the Lizard Clan, the tail going with the Snake." With this act the gods left the earth and the people were scattered. Soon "mistrust and hatred" were all over. Then one day a group living on the high mesa had a vision telling them that the two parts of the snake would be reunited and that "the people would be swept from the earth by a star, for they were to be saved from the destruction at hand." When Mickey asks what he should do, the Spider Lady replies, "You must see the truth of this myth I have told you." From this point, there is a clear opposition between Mickey Free's desire for the transcendent and the reconciliatory and both the government's and the revolutionaries' commitment to the immediate and the confrontational.

The penultimate scene of the play satirizes the political paranoia of the establishment. Captain Bovine, chief inspector for the CIA, interrogates Billy and warns him against the subversives who are threatening America. He tells Billy of "a breakdown of law and order and a complete disrespect for the things we've held sacred since our ancestors founded this country" and confides that is time to "root out these subversive, underground creeps and wipe the slate clean once and for all." During the interrogation, Billy uses the word *sidewinder*, and Dr. Vector, who is also present, immediately perks up. When Billy mentions that he has seen the sidewinder, Dr. Vector becomes ecstatic and, using lines from the movie *Dr. Frankenstein*, yells, "It's alive! My sidewinder is alive! It lives! It lives!" Billy also reveals that he has the bags of dope that the young man had given to Mickey Free, which Mickey had given to him to return to "the white devil." In response Bovine calls for "a special detail of Desert Tactical Troops." The scene blacks out, and the song "C.I.A. Man" is heard:

Who can tell if Egypt's got the bomb . . .
Who can train guerillas by the dozen . . .
Who can plant the bug on anyone . . .
Who will do just what he has to do . . .
Fuckin A Man C.I.A. Man.

The play ends in an extraordinary Hopi-inspired ritual based on the Ceremony of the Snake and Antelope Fraternities. The elaborate dance, which occurs on the sixteenth and last day of the ceremony, demands that the participants take live rattlesnakes in their mouths as an "exhibition of manliness and fearlessness."[2] *Operation Sidewinder* recreates elements of this dance in great detail and with the utmost seriousness. "Everything about the dance is spiritual and sincere," counsels Shepard in the stage directions, "and should not be cartooned or choreographed beyond the unison of the rhythmic patterns."

Into the middle of this ceremony come Honey and the young man, carrying the body of the sidewinder and looking for Mickey Free. Mickey has completely changed from his former self and greets the young man as the one who has brought them their salvation since the body of the side-

2. Edward S. Curtis, *The North American Indian*, vol. 12 (New York: Johnson Reprint Corporation, 1970), p. 145.

winder can now be reunited with the head. He invites Honey and the young man to make the spiritual transition to another world, but the young man only wants to leave. Honey gets drawn into the ceremony, however, and walks, in a trancelike state, into Mickey Free's wikiup. The young man soon follows, and the two of them eventually emerge in Indian costume with painted bodies.

The ceremony is interrupted with the arrival of three Desert Tactical troops. When the Indians refuse to obey their order to stop the ceremony and hand over the sidewinder, the troops open fire, but to no avail. The Indians keep moving, gusts of wind blow across the stage, and streams of smoke flow in from around the proscenium and the upstage area. The lights go to black and then come up in blue; the Indians, Honey, and the young man are gone. The power of the ritual has completely transcended political confrontation.

Shepard's fascination with the Hopi, and with Indian culture in general, plays an important part in his writing. We have seen it in the identification of his birth with the Hopi Hawk Moon month, in the Indian ghost that haunts Pop in *The Holy Ghostly*, and now in the complex and elaborately staged Snake and Antelope ritual in *Operation Sidewinder*. The power of ritual to transform experience can also be found in a particularly pungent example in a short prose piece entitled "Left Handed Kachina," which Shepard included in the collection *Hawk Moon*. It tells about a tourist couple who buy a Kachina doll from a young Hopi who lives in a tar paper shack near the ancient settlement of Old Oraibi in Arizona. When they get back to New York City, the Kachina begins to control the husband and finally reduces him to an animallike state and changes his apartment into a storm-swept landscape.

For Shepard the power of ritual and the power of words are linked. Citing American Indian poetry as an example, he has described a kind of religious belief in words: "Words as living incantations and not as symbols. Taken in this way, the organization of living, breathing words as they hit the air between the actor and the audience actually possess the power to change our chemistry." It is this power that is literalized in "Left Handed Kachina" and that stands behind what Shepard has called "the real quest of a writer . . . to penetrate into another world . . . behind the form."[3]

Shepard's first venture uptown into the world of official theater was not well received by the critics. Nevertheless, *Operation Sidewinder*, with its large cast and complex staging requirements, could not have been done in the theaters to which Shepard had become accustomed and in which the most adventurous audiences were to be found. With his next production, however, Shepard returned to the more open and accepting world of Off Off Broadway. On 20 July 1970 *Shaved Splits* opened at La Mama Experimental Theatre Club, which already had housed four Shepard plays.

Shaved Splits concludes what might be called a trilogy on revolution that includes *Forensic and the Navigators* and *Operation Sidewinder*. Structurally, it has more in common with *Forensic*, while in terms of character it is closer to *Sidewinder*. All three present revolutionary activity in an American context as problematic at best. *Forensic* leaves its activists hiding under a table, along with one of the Exterminators who originally came to wipe them out. With new agents of authority banging at the door, the 2nd Exterminator, who also has walked out on the system, can only stand immobilized, refusing ever to go outside again. *Sidewinder* presents a way out of the impasse of frustrated and confused political activity, but only in mystical terms that make most sense in the radically different context of traditional Hopi culture. *Shaved Splits* simply abandons the confrontation with the established order and declares the war to be over, finding salvation for its revolutionary character not in transcendence but in the more down-to-earth realm of rock and roll.

Shaves Splits is essentially a play of fantasies. It begins in "the bedroom chambers of the Castle Cherry." Miss Cherry twists voluptuously in her bed reading pornography and eating chocolates, while in the streets below revolution

3. "Language, Visualization, and the Inner Library," pp. 216–17.

rages. During the opening minutes, however, Cherry's private, sensual concerns dominate. The first words are those of Cherry reading from her pornographic book, aggressively broadcast to the audience over the theater's public-address system. Her fantasy interrupted by a part in her book that even she finds disgusting, she calls her servant Wong, ordering him to tell her porno supplier, Chunky Puke, never to bring anything like that again.

Cherry's sexual fantasies are linked to a social fantasy that causes her to treat Wong as a possession among her other possessions. As she reminds him, "I got a rich influential husband, plenty of money, a yacht, no, two yachts, a Jaguar XKE, an Alfa Romeo, a Mini Cooper, a Fiat Abarth, a Ford Cobra and a lot of other stuff." She calls Wong a "dumb chink," and when she tries to use him sexually and he resists, she complains that her husband, D. T., has "hired a bunch a' faggot servants." Opening the window and looking out on the action in the streets below, she yells the standard phrase of the sixties defenders of the status quo, though she adds to it an epithet befitting her character: "America! Love it or leave it, motherfuckers!"

To this duality of political conservatism and addiction to pornography, Shepard adds a strain of sadism, exemplified in her reading from a book in which a man "lay in the red clay with his belly ripped open and the guts pouring down both his legs." Out of this nexus of sensuality and aggression, Cherry verbalizes an ideology of self-interest and personal comfort: "This is a fucked up country. . . . A schizophrenic country. Split right up the middle. It's never gotten together and it never will. Thing is you gotta make sense out of all the chaos or else you're up shit creek. . . . You gotta make yourself a personal world where things work the way they're supposed to. Where you're comfy and warm."

Into this personal world bursts Geez, a young revolutionary with wounds on the head and leg. The guerrilla plans of *Forensic* and *Sidewinder* have turned into armed insurrection; the worst fears of Captain Bovine have been realized. "I've killed about fourteen people today," Geez warns Cherry. "At first it was a little traumatic. . . . But now I know I can do it. Any time, anywhere." For Geez, however, the battle is drawing to a close. The police know he is there and demand his surrender. He responds defiantly in the same terms that Cherry has used in relation to Wong and the revolutionaries: "This is me, motherfucker! If you want me, come up and get me, you stupid pig bastard faggots." The more Geez and Cherry talk, the more similar they seem. He calls her husband a faggot, as she herself did earlier, and when she, contrary to her own remarks, tries to defend him, Geez says, "Who gives a rat's ass!" Cherry gave the same response to one of the books she was reading before her apartment was invaded.

Both Cherry and Geez are obsessed people, and Shepard draws little distinction between their obsessions. This quality is emphasized by Wong, who reenters at one point wearing a Chinese dragon mask and ritual costume and begins dancing in complete oblivion to what is going on around him. To this three-ring circus, Shepard adds Cherry's husband, who arrives by helicopter. He launches into a controlled harangue against Geez and his "vain inane ideology," which hopes that "a cause might win over a concrete reality." When Cherry tells him to shut up and accuses him of being worse than Geez, D. T. responds that, in fact, they are the same, they both are "wrapped up in a losing struggle against reality." Geez rejects this analysis, but D. T.'s remarks reveal that he too is an obsessed personality, obsessed by money, by the acquisition of things, and, as are the other characters, by his own personal concerns and perspective on reality.

After D. T. finishes his speech, Cherry demands that he do something about their predicament. He runs to the window to shout for help but gets shot by the police. With D. T. dying, Cherry begs Geez to take her away with him, only to be told that there is no place to go. Geez suggests that the only safe place is under the bed, and, like the characters in *Forensic*, she shuts herself off from what is going on. At that point Wong stops dancing, stares momentarily at Geez, and jumps out the window, taking his obsession to its limit. D. T. begins talking about himself, about the ambition and talent he once had, which somehow got lost in the corporation. Geez sits back to wait for the final confrontation, saying it is like the stillness that accompanies deer hunting. Each continues without any regard to the other, while Cherry periodically asks if it is safe to come out from under the bed. Finally, Cherry wants to know what is going on, and Geez answers simply, "The war's over."

This remark introduces the final fantasy, which, like Cherry's pornographic fantasy that began the play, is narrated over the public-address system. Geez's voice is heard as he describes himself in the third person walking across the rubble of the postwar city. There are no more crowds of people or movie theaters or boxes of popcorn, just "everywhere the stench of the dead and the dying." Then, "somewhere in his mind" he hears a band playing, with Chuck Berry, Elvis Presley, Little Richard, the Rolling Stones, and Fats Domino all blending into one. He follows the music into the backroom of a burned-out bar, and there on the bandstand is a group playing "Satisfaction." Although he does not know how to play, he picks up an electric guitar and joins in. "The music filled him up and poured out over the dusty tables and chairs. He was alive again. The war was over and he was alive."

Despite everything that has been said about the political context of *Forsenic and the Navigators*, *Operation Sidewinder*, and *Shaved Splits*, the desire of the revolutionary to overthrow the established order can also be seen as the perfect metaphor for the role of the artist. For Shepard, art is always a matter of new beginnings, of struggling not only against established forms but also against his own accomplishments and audiences' perceptions of them. "It becomes more and more difficult to write something surprising or in a new way because people now come with expectations—they expect it will be about 'the myth of America' or something. Once you've cracked the beginning, you're on a roll, but it gets more difficult to start. You've got to get rid of all the stuff in your head that you've done before in order to start off from ground zero, and for me, that's the only place to start."[4]

The specific forms of this struggle and the responses they generate vary in each of the three plays and, to a degree, parallel developments in Shepard's career. In *Forensic*, the revolutionary/artist figure is split into Forensic and Emmet, one of whom wants to go ahead at all costs and the other of whom wants to reevaluate tactics. In the face of possible extermination, they hide under the table, unable to resolve the contradictions and conflicts inherent in their endeavor. Perhaps significantly, this play immediately precedes a two-year period during which Shepard produced no new plays. At the end of that period, Forensic and Emmet reemerge under new names in *Operation Sidewinder*. Again, the artist as revolutionary is split in two: the young man, who under the influence of drugs and violent frustrations struggles with being an alien in his own country, and Mickey Free, who by returning to ancient myths and rituals seeks a spiritual renewal. A few months later, in *Shaved Splits*, the anger and frustration of the young man have reached new levels in Geez, while the desire for transcendence has been redirected to the hope of salvation through music. Shepard's experience as drummer in the Holy Modal Rounders, the increasing importance of music in his plays, and the changing nature of the New York theater scene seemed to be moving him away from writing into the fantasy of becoming a rock star, so much so that in 1971, along with his wife O-Lan and his son Jesse, he moved to England "to get into music." Before doing so, however, he wrote three more plays, each of which uses music as an important element.

On 4 March 1971, Theatre Genesis, which had launched Shepard's career with its productions of *Cowboys* and *The Rock Garden*, premiered *The Mad Dog Blues*. Modeling his play partly on John Huston's film *Treasure of the Sierra Madre*, Shepard subtitled it "A Two-Act Adventure Show" and endowed it with the kind of freedom of space and time that is largely the province of the movies. What director

4. *New York Times*, 29 January 1984, section 2, p. 26.

Michael McClure once wrote about *Operation Sidewinder* applies equally well to *The Mad Dog Blues*: "Action and novelty are brought back to the stage."[5]

The far-ranging action is presented without scenery and with only a few props, allowing for maximum imaginative participation by the audience. Sound effects and music are to be performed live, with the band situated in the pit area "as for a vaudeville show." The characters signify a diverse range of cultural meanings: Kosmo, a rock-and-roll star with tight pants and teased hair; Yahoodi, a junkie who dresses "like a big-city dope dealer"; Waco, a guitar-carrying drifter in cowboy clothes; Marlene Dietrich and Mae West living up to their movie images; Captain Kidd in swashbuckling outfit; Paul Bunyan on a perpetual search for his ox Babe; Jesse James, a true representative of the myth of the old West; and Ghost Girl, a South Sea islander.

The play begins with a brief prologue in which Kosmo and Yahoodi, speaking from "opposite sides of the stage . . . and directly to the audience," describe themselves from their own perspectives. Taken together they encompass different and sometimes contradictory aspects of a single personality that suggest Shepard himself at that period in his life. Kosmo: "Tall, lean, angular, wolflike . . . intuitive. . . . Lots of dashing images. . . . Has no control over his primeval violence. . . . Moves from spot to spot . . . hoping to find a home." Yahoodi: "Loves how the brain works. Sucks in the printed word. Prefers isolation. . . . Trades his mojo for a bag of coke and disappears in the night." The musician and the writer. The man of action and the observer. The emotional and the intellectual. Sidekicks, sometimes going their separate ways but searching for a unified vision.

Kosmo and Yahoodi begin their search separated by a vast expanse, the undefined space of the bare stage articulated only by light. Kosmo calls to Yahoodi and tells him of a vision, which came to him like an old rhythm-and-blues song with a Jimi Hendrix lead line, accompanied by

5. Michael McClure, "Introduction," in Sam Shepard, *Mad Dog Blues and Other Plays* (New York: Winter House, Ltd., 1972), p. 1.

an image of Marlene Dietrich in short shorts. But the city is getting him down, and he cannot sing it. As with Shepard in New York at this time, there are too many tangents; Kosmo has to go somewhere. He decides on San Francisco, while Yahoodi heads for the jungle. Marlene Dietrich, whose presence was called up by Kosmo's vision, goes into the audience and sings about young men searching for themselves who will not find anything until they find their own hearts.

Kosmo has a second vision, "Mae West singing the blues like Janis Joplin." The past joins with the present again and Kosmo is inspired: "Jack Kerouac country! The Grateful Dead. The Airplane, Quicksilver. The air is full of grist for the mill." He feels like he is "getting closer and closer to the truth." If he could only "put something together." He asks Mae West to take him for a trolley ride, and she responds, "I'll take ya for everything ya got." Kosmo comments on how much smaller she is in real life than in the movies.

Breaking into Kosmo's flood of images, Yahoodi calls from the jungle. He needs some dope, just a little something to keep him going, but Kosmo does not hear. His friend having failed him, he is visited by Marlene Dietrich, who tries to comfort him with sex. Neither Mae nor Marlene, however, can satisfy the deeper needs of the two travelers.

Once again Yahoodi calls to Kosmo. He tells of a dream in which he was Crazy Horse leading a raid against the Crows; for the first time he knew what it was like to be without fear. Kosmo, still in his own world, describes a journey to see his father, only to find his home a ghost town and his father unable to recognize him. For a third time Yahoodi calls to Kosmo, but this time Kosmo comes to him. Yahoodi recounts another vision: an American bald eagle drops the world into the ocean, causing it to explode and to send up a giant tidal wave. This image, which recalls the plane crash in *Red Cross* and which looks forward to a story told in *Curse of the Starving Class*, elicits from Kosmo a rejection of its political meaning: "I'm getting fucking tired of apocalypses. All I ever hear anymore is apocalypse, apocalypse. What about something with some hope?"

On one level, the rest of the play is a search for that hope, a search for personal wholeness amid social and political fragmentation. The vehicle for this search is the *Treasure of Sierra Madre* adventure format, which brings Kosmo and Yahoodi together with characters from history, myth, and the movies in an odyssey through a complicated montage of imaginative landscapes.

The adventure begins with an invocation. Glad that he is out of the States, Yahoodi pictures himself hunting for gold, but he is not quite sure how to start. "If I could just find Humphrey Bogart we'd be in business," he tells Marlene. Since Kosmo has already conjured up Dietrich and West, the appearance of Bogart would not be surprising. However, it is the existential toughness and independence of the Bogart persona that Yahoodi needs and not the man himself. Yahoodi does not have these qualities, but, as he indicates by invoking the name, he does hold an idealized conception of them that can lead to action. Like the teenage Sam Shepard pretending to be Burt Lancaster, Yahoodi takes inspiration from the movies and acts on it.

In keeping with *Treasure of the Sierra Madre*, the action of *The Mad Dog Blues* is set "South of the Border." Although Yahoodi has gone to an undefined jungle, he speaks of buying mules in Nogales; later, Mae worries about being caught by the Federales. When Kosmo leaves San Francisco to join Yahoodi in the gold search, he heads south, the direction of danger, of the exotic, of possibility. "I've always been pulled toward darkness," wrote Shepard. "Toward black. Toward death. Toward the South."[6] Like the characters in the Huston film, Yahoodi and Kosmo find themselves ensnared in an intrigue of violence, greed, and betrayal that threatens to separate them even more than they already are and that finally causes Yahoodi to shoot himself.

Almost immediately, Yahoodi's desire to dig for gold gets sidetracked into a hunt for pirate treasure when he en-

6. *Hawk Moon*, pp. 49–50.

counters Captain Kidd. Ultimately, the treasure turns out to be worthless bags of bottle caps, but not until Yahoodi and Kosmo have been talked into betraying each other. In and out of this tale of gold lust wanders the folklore figure of Paul Bunyan as a representative of certain simple virtues. "You city slickers are always looking to buy and sell things," he tells Yahoodi and Marlene. For his part, he is only looking for his ox, Babe, and he wants no part of the treasure hunt.

Although Yahoodi and Kosmo are involved in the treasure hunt, they are not in it for the gold as are Captain Kidd, Marlene, and Mae. Their search is of a spiritual nature; their presence in the jungle is a sign of their alienation from American society. But it is an alienation born out of an inescapable connection. When Yahoodi is aboard Kidd's ship, he looks through a telescope to see if they are being followed, but instead of seeing pursuers or empty ocean, he sees "the whole world going up in smoke." He also sees "two men on a raft eating Tootsie Rolls," a possible reference to Charlie Mingus, Jr., and Shepard during their early days in New York before life became complicated by both artistic success and the social and political turmoil of the late sixties. Patti Smith said of Shepard in that period that he "wrote his first play *Cowboys* in true pioneer style . . . on the back of used Tootsie Roll wrappers."[7] Kosmo, following in another boat, hears things that Mae, who is with him, cannot. He hears the music of Jimi Hendrix and Janis Joplin and the voices of "thousands of people screaming." For Yahoodi and Kosmo, America is a place that is both hard to live in and hard to leave.

Near the beginning of act 2, Kosmo states his real need very directly. "I just wanna find my roots," he declares to Mae. "I can't hear the music anymore. I can't hear the band." When Mae responds that with his share of the treasure he will be able to buy a dozen bands, he insists, "I want *my* band. I don't want a dozen bands. I just wanna play my music. My own special music." Receiving no positive reinforcement from Mae, who calls him "a rock-and-

7. "Sam Shepard," p. 155.

roll punk," Kosmo calls out to Yahoodi, "I had a vision! Jimi Hendrix and Janis Joplin and Buddy Holly and Sam Cooke and Big Bopper and Otis Redding and Brian Jones and Jimmie Rodgers and Blind Lemon Jefferson! They're all in heaven and they've started a band!" Kosmo recognizes that his musical roots and his individual style are linked, just as the musicians he names each has his own style though they play together in the same heavenly band.

Lying behind Kosmo's affirmation of his musical heritage is the larger issue of the relationship between an artist and the culture that has nourished him. After spending three years in England, Shepard concluded that he could not "be anything other than an American writer," just as Kosmo, after identifying some of his roots, cries out, "I wanna go home. I wanna see my wife and kids again." The desire cannot be simply fulfilled, however, and Kosmo is fated to continue his alienated relationship with home. "But which way is home?" he asks Mae. "I don't know where to start. . . . I'm lost."

While Kosmo concerns himself with these issues of identity and home, Yahoodi is engaged in a life-and-death struggle with Captain Kidd over possession of the gold. Getting the upper hand, Yahoodi shoots Kidd, only to have his own fear and madness cause him to turn the gun on himself. Kosmo, who has been following Yahoodi, hears the shot and arrives to find his friend lying on top of the treasure. While he agonizes, Mae grabs the treasure. Just then Jesse James enters to rob them. Mae makes a deal with him, however: "We split the dough fifty-fifty and I'll let ya come up and see me sometime." The movie legend proves more potent than the historical legend, and they go off together, leaving Kosmo behind to deal with Yahoodi and the problem of the plot.

Not sure what to do next, Kosmo pauses and "looks around the stage." In this case, Shepard's directions are to be taken quite literally, Kosmo looks around the stage and not around the jungle. At Shepard's bidding, he acknowledges the real space in which the action is taking place, the space of the theater, and, without any regard for the illusion of story, he addresses Yahoodi: "All right, all right. You can get up now. . . . Look, it's not going to work out if you go and off yourself right when everything gets going so good. . . . We got all these characters strung out all over the place in all these different lives and you just go and rub yourself out. . . . Is that responsible? . . . If you don't want to go through with this thing then just tell me. . . . But don't kill yourself off in the middle of the plot." Yahoodi sits up and argues with Kosmo over the quality of the story and characters. The argument moves beyond this narrow subject to the larger question of their relationship. Kosmo talks about his angels, and Yahoodi about his demons. "I'm struggling with something in me that wants to die!" says Yahoodi. "And I'm struggling with something that wants to live," counters Kosmo. To this impasse, there is no resolution, so they split up once again.

As the play nears its conclusion, the various characters wander around in search of each other, but for the most part they miss each other or get lost. Kosmo and Yahoodi have one brief, final encounter in which Kosmo complains that things are getting worse, that everything is crashing in on him. Only Mae and Jesse James remain together, an oddly appropriate couple, each independent, courageous, and tough minded, two American renegades who are also heroes. With the Federales pursuing them, they are heading for the border with the remaining bags of gold. "If we only had us a horse," laments Mae. Just then Paul Bunyan's missing blue ox Babe enters; Mae and Jesse mount him and ride crashing through U.S. Customs to safety.

They have returned to the States only to discover that their treasure is nothing but bottle caps. In need of a new goal, Jesse suggests that they go to Missouri and see his family. Mae at first objects that she is not "much of a family gal," but soon likes the idea, so much so that she wants to gather all the others and take them to Missouri as well. "Wouldn't that be something though?" she asks. "All of us comin' into town. . . . All of us singin' and dancin' and carrying' on. . . . Just like the old days. Just like the new days! . . . Let's do it Jesse! Let's go home! Back where we belong!" Then, in a grand finale, all the characters join in a song about home, dance around, and march "through the audience and out into the street."

Although the simplicity of the ending belies the confussions and contradictions that have motivated the characters throughout, it is also meant to be taken seriously as a projection of a fundamental need, not in the least weakened by the problematic nature of the very home that is desired. While describing this need and the general confusion of the times, Shepard provides no solutions. It is enough for him to give a feeling for a time in which loss is the primal condition of being and in which there is a longing on the part of many to walk to the sound of their own music.

Shepard's next play, cowritten with rock singer Patti Smith, was *Cowboy Mouth*. In its story of a man imprisoned by contradictory desires, it is a companion piece to *The Mad Dog Blues*, reuniting in the character of Slim the personality traits and conflicting motivations of Kosmo and Yahoodi. Its setting, however, is as defined and cluttered with cultural signs as that of *The Mad Dog Blues* is undefined and spare. The entire action takes place in one room during a brief period "after one too many mornings." A well-used, rumpled bed in center stage provides a focal point for much of the action, recalling *Red Cross*, *La Turista*, and especially *Shaved Splits* and looking forward to *Geography of a Horse Dreamer* and *Fool for Love*. Debris of various kinds covers the floor, and on the walls are peeling pictures of cowboys and photographs of country-and-western singers Hank Williams and Jimmie Rodgers. On one side of the stage is a set of drums and on the other are an electric guitar and amplifier.

In *Cowboy Mouth* Shepard treated ironically his professed desire to be a rock star, at the same time creating another portrait of the personal and artistic confusion that would soon cause him to seek a fresh start in England. Like Kosmo and Yahoodi, Slim begins the play chafing under a sense of confinement. Cavale had kidnapped him at gunpoint in order to make a rock-and-roll savior out of him, and although he stayed because he too had a similar dream, he now wants out. He accuses her of stealing him away from his wife and baby, of tempting him into sin, and, worst of all, of causing him not to know who he is anymore. She counters by explaining the meaning of her action. "The highest form of anything is sainthood," she tells him. "A marvellous thief like Villon or Genêt . . . they were saints 'cause they raised thievery to its highest state of grace. . . . Some say Jesse James was one . . . and . . . I dream of being one. But I can't. . . . People want a street angel. They want a saint but with a cowboy mouth. . . . A sort of god in our image." She then links this notion to the importance of rock and roll in her life. Echoing Shepard's comment on rock and roll in *Hawk Moon*, she ascribes a religious function to the music and a special place to the rock-and-roll star:

> We're earthy people and the old saints just don't make it and the old God is just too far away. . . . His words don't shake through us no more. Any great motherfucker rock-n'-roll song can raise me higher than all of Revelations. We created rock-n'-roll from our own image, it's our child . . . a child that's gotta burst in the mouth of a savior. . . . It's like . . . the rock-n'-roll star in his highest state of grace will be the new savior.

Although Slim objects that he is no savior, Cavale insists that he can become one, that he has "the magic." Her prescription as to how he should go about being the rock-and-roll savior is the very one that would heal the fragmentation and alienation suffered by Kosmo and Yahoodi, and since they are united in Slim, it is also the way in which he can heal himself. "You gotta reach out and grab all the little broken busted-up pieces of people's frustration. That stuff in them that's lookin' for a way out or a way in. . . . And then you gotta take all that into yourself and pour it back out. Give it back to them bigger than life." In effect, Cavale has described not only the function of a savior but also the function of an artist. She has challenged Slim (and Shepard?) to be the artist that he is, to succeed in getting together what Kosmo felt he was getting close to but was never able to achieve.

96

Feeling trapped by this challenge, Slim reacts violently and curses Cavale for bringing his "dream up to the surface like that." But it is her dream, not his, that is at stake, and she responds to his self-pity with stinging sarcasm:

> I spread my dreams at your feet, everything I believe in, and you tread all over them with your simpy horseshit. . . . Poor poor baby. I take your world and shake it. Well, you took my fantasy and shit on it. I . . . was looking for a man with nothing so I could give him everything. Everything it takes to make the world reel like a drunkard. But you have less than nothing, baby, you have part of a thing.

Cavale's put-down of Slim brings him up short, but it also reveals a conflict that makes her as much a prisoner as Slim. Just as Slim is drawn to the dream of being the rock-and-roll savior and is in love with Cavale but at the same time wants to escape the dream's demands and return to his wife, so Cavale is committed to creating the savior while realizing all the time that the whole thing is a fantasy. Shepard's move to England was at least partly inspired by the dreams and fantasies he ascribes to Slim and Cavale. To a British interviewer, he confided, "I was in a band in New York, and I'd heard that this was the rock 'n' roll center of the world—so I came here with that kind of idea. London was notorious for its rock 'n' roll bands, . . . so I had this fantasy that I'd come over here and somehow fall into a rock 'n' roll band. It didn't work."[8]

The contradictions and confused feelings that Slim and Cavale express throughout are summed up at the end of the play in the song "Loose Ends." Cavale begins to talk the song while Slim accompanies on the guitar: "I'm at loose ends / I don't know what to do / Always dreaming big dreams . . . / To tell the truth I don't know which way to turn/ Give me something to hold on to." Her lament, which recalls the feelings expressed by Kosmo in *The Mad Dog Blues*, is then answered in the chorus, which Slim sings with Cavale: "Come right here when you feel alone / And no one speaks for you / You can do it on your own." This self-help ethic, seen earlier in the song "Prisoners, Get

8. Chubb, "Metaphors," p. 200.

up out of Your Homemade Beds" from *Melodrama Play*, and echoing advice that Yahoodi gives Kosmo at their final meeting, is the only solution that the play offers for escape from personal and artistic constraints. It causes Cavale to change in the third verse to the past tense and to sing rather than talk when she once again picks up the song's lead line: "Oh I was at loose ends / Not knowing what to do / I needed to open up / So I turned to you." The result is a bringing down to earth of the dreams that were too high to be accomplished: "Down on the ground / Where I can feel it / Where I can touch it / Where I can be it."

The play's third character, the Lobster Man, was introduced earlier. As his name implies, he is a man dressed like a lobster, who on his first appearance performs the practical function of delivering lobster that Slim and Cavale have ordered. He is also present while "Loose Ends" is being performed, during which time he slowly cracks open his shell to reveal himself as the rock-and-roll savior. No longer needed for the part, Slim can now leave, but before he does, he hands the Lobster Man Cavale's gun, which she had originally used to kidnap him. As the Lobster Man stands spinning the chamber of the gun, Cavale tells him about Nerval, the French artist/criminal who used to carry a crow and lead a pet lobster on a pink ribbon and who hung himself on Cavale's birthday. "The moon was cold and full and his visions and the crow and the lobster went on *cavale*. That's where I found my name Cavale. On my birthday. It means escape." As Cavale concludes her story, the Lobster Man puts the gun to his head and pulls the trigger. It clicks on an empty chamber, and the lights fade to black.

Nerval, like Genet and Villon, was another candidate for artist/savior, but he could no more fulfill the demands of the part than could Slim, who finally escapes, or Cavale (or Patti Smith?), whose very name defines her position, or the Lobster Man, who ultimately will lose his game of Russian roulette. Saviors come and go, and for every successful artist, the pressure to become one is both a temptation and a trap. More important, however, is that in the play's terms the concept of savior itself is questionable. As the final verse of "Loose Ends" puts it, "If you got no savior you can do it on your own / Open up your heart don't think about a thing / Feel the movement in you and sing." If everyone can do it on his own, then everyone is a savior.

Cowboy Mouth is a remarkable play. It summarizes the themes of freedom, confinement, personal responsibility, and self-help introduced in several of the earlier, more expansive plays, examines with both passion and objectivity the experiences that Shepard himself was going through at the time, and almost entirely shifts the burden of drama to the power of language. Unlike *The Mad Dog Blues*, which depends heavily on its sense of space and movement, *Cowboy Mouth* is predominantly interior. The verbal battles, the cluttered landscape of the apartment, and the physical appearance of the characters, which Shepard graphically describes as "beat to shit," are the specific signs of the contradictions raging within Slim and Cavale. As a result, the play also marks Shepard's first intensive exploration of character and points to some of his most recent work, especially *True West* and *Fool for Love*.

On the same program with the American Place Theatre's production of *Cowboy Mouth* was Shepard's last play before leaving for England, *Back Bog Beast Bait*. It is a striking blend of Bible-inspired allegory and Western melodrama, punctuated with songs by Shepard, Lou Reed, Steve Weber, and Antonia. In its apocalpytic intensity, it would have caused much distress for poor Kosmo could he have seen it, searching as he was for something with hope. *Back Bog Beast Bait* contains little if any hope; its characters are the bait for the beast, and Slim, its potential hero, is absorbed by a force beyond his control. Unlike *The Mad Dog Blues* or *Cowboy Mouth*, there is no possibility of returning home or of escaping, though like them it is a blues play in which the dominant image is one of entrapment and the need to escape.

The play opens with a song sung in the darkness:

> I got those boxed in back bog blues,
> I know you heard them, they ain't nothin' new. . . .
> I need more than three squares and a bed,
> I gots to take care of the state of my head . . .

If I had me a Ford or a Cadillac,
I'd be out of here and I would never come back. . . .
But there's one thing that worries me,
If I go back, who's gonna recognize me?

Although sung by Ghost Girl, the image applies to Slim, a gunfighter who is past his prime and who has "nightmares a' bein' gunned down on the street by some a' these hot shot young dudes that a' been sproutin' up." Traveling with Slim is Shadow, a younger gunfighter who may be one of the "hot shot young dudes" that Slim is afraid of. Together they have been hired by Maria, a pregnant Mexican woman, to protect her and her son from the Tarpin, the pig beast, which has already castrated all the other boys in the bayou and wants to kill her to prevent her from giving birth. When Maria describes the beast, Shadow tries to explain its appearance in a rational way. "Maybe it is an Arapaho in some kinda' crazy costume," he suggests. Slim, on the other hand, sees in the beast something deeper and essentially unexplainable. Like Pop in *The Holy Ghostly*, he is moved by undefinable fears. "Nope, it's somethin' bigger and spookier than you or me can reckon to," he tells Shadow. "Somethin's goin' on down here, Shadow. Somethin' horrible's goin' on." Unmoved by Slim's speculation, Shadow goes for a walk in the moonlight hoping to find a willing Cajun girl. Slim beds down and delivers a monologue on the loneliness of his life, at the end of which the Ghost Girl enters and sings about a dream of the earth sinking into the sea.

The next morning Shadow returns with a Cajun girl named Gris Gris and an armful of big yellow mushrooms, which he claims they picked on a mountain. Shadow continues to scoff at the idea of a beast and eats a mushroom despite Slim's warning that they may be poisonous and may even be bait put out by the beast. Soon Shadow doubles up in pain, and Gris Gris reveals herself as a witch who can call up the beast. She tells Slim that the beast is in him. She raises Slim's fear of other gunfighters who are after him, a fear that is linked to the threat of the beast, eventually driving him out of the shack in a search for the mysterious mountain of the mushrooms. With Slim gone, Gris Gris launches into an elaborate, surreal, apocalyptic vision of the coming of the beast. As she wails, "The beast is come," his two heads appear in the windows of the shack, Shadow falls lifeless, and Maria discovers that her son has been killed.

The tone of the final scene is set by a song filled with apocalyptic visions of an almost medieval character. Slim returns to confront Gris Gris but discovers that his once "incredible power to kill" has left him. Gris Gris taunts him while Maria recites passages from the Book of Revelation about the woman clothed with the sun who is about to give birth and whose child is threatened by the great red dragon. Slim pleads to the beast not to be taken yet, and as he does so, he begins to turn into a coyote. Finally, he calls out, "I am the beast. The beast is me." Simultaneously, all the other characters turn into animals, moving and uttering sounds in appropriate fashion.

Just before the transformation into animals concludes, the Tarpin bursts through the door into the middle of a scene in which each character is totally involved in his own ritual, so much so that none of them notices the Tarpin. With the beast inside each one of them so clearly in evidence, the actual pig beast has become irrelevant. His dreaded arrival is anticlimatic, and so he exits, "helpless and alone in the situation." In contrast to the rock-and-roll savior of *Cowboy Mouth*, who may, in fact, be inside everyone, *Back Bog Beast Bait* presents the image of the beast of Revelation, whose number is also the "number of man," and whose fearsome countenance is our own. The famous line from Yeats quoted by Slim in *Cowboy Mouth* is doubly relevant here: "what rough beast . . . / Slouches towards Bethlehem to be born?"

For the artist, Yeats's question is a perpetual one, whether it applies to life in general or to the place and function of the artist in particular. It is a question that is given another literal manifestation in the first play that Shepard wrote after moving with his wife and son to England. The distance he gained from the New York theater and from American society, where the gap between living

101

and working was becoming wider and wider, gave him a perspective on his work and his life that helped set the stage for the most original and powerful work he had yet produced, *The Tooth of Crime*. "It wasn't until I came to England," he told an interviewer, "that I found out what it means to be an American. Nothing really makes sense when you're there, but the more distant you are from it, the more the implications of what you grew up with start to emerge."[9]

One of the things that emerged was a heightened sense of the underlying violence of American society. This awareness had always been present in Shepard's work, but in *The Tooth of Crime* it took on a particularly virulent form. "The character of Crow . . . came from a yearning toward violence," wrote Shepard. "A totally lethal human with no way or reason for tracing how he got that way. . . . He spit words that became his weapons. . . . He speaks in an unheard-of tongue. He needed a victim, so I gave him one. He devoured him just like he was supposed to."[10] Crow's immediate model is the young Western gunslinger out to kill the old-timer with the reputation as the fastest on the draw, but as an archetype he is as old as myth itself. He is Cain hating Abel and the aspirant to the office of priest/king who kills his predecessor in the darkness of the primeval forest. He is also the contemporary American who out of fear or boredom or frustration reaches for a gun: "Any gun. A blue gun. A fast gun. A slow gun. A gun fight. A good fast gun fight. A Winchester, lever action 30.30. Now there's a gun to take care of anything. They look good too. Make you feel good to hold one. Like a cowboy again."[11]

The Tooth of Crime is a rock-and-roll Western set in a futuristic present, in a world defined by the language and ethics of the music industry. The action takes place on a bare stage, with a silver-studded high-back chair, "like an Egyptian Pharaoh's throne," the only prop. As the play begins, a hidden band plays "heavy lurking Rock and Roll"

9. Ibid., p. 198.
10. "Language, Visualization, and the Inner Library," p. 217.
11. *Hawk Moon*, p. 54.

in the dark. The lights come up and Hoss, a top rock star who looks like a young, "mean Rip Torn," enters wearing "black rocker gear with silver studs and black kid gloves." Microphone in hand, he sings the first of a series of songs that comment on the action and give emotional distance to the audience's feelings. Like the chorus in Shakespeare's *Henry V*, Hoss steps forward and warns the audience about the illusory nature of what they are about to see:

> You may think every picture you see is a true history
> of the way things used to be or the way things are
> While you're ridin' in your radio or walkin' through
> the late late show ain't it a drag to know you just don't
> know
> you just don't know
> So here's another illusion to add to your confusion
> Of the way things are . . .
> So here's another sleep-walkin' dream
> A livin' talkin' show of the way things seem
> I used to believe in rhythm and blues
> Always wore my blue suede shoes
> Now everything I do goes down in doubt . . .
> So here's another fantasy
> About the way things seem to be to me.

As soon as he finishes, Hoss throws down the microphone, and the action of the play commences.

Hoss is at the top of the charts, but like the old gunfighter of the classic Western, he is constantly being stalked by newcomers. Star-Man, Hoss's top-forty-chart astrologer, warns him not to make a wrong move. "The charts are moving too fast," he tells him. "Every week there's a new star." But Hoss is anxious to make a new kill. The teleprompters have already reported that Mojo Rootforce has knocked over Vegas, which used to be Hoss's mark. Hoss talks about wiping him out, but Becky and Star-Man, who function as Hoss's promoters, restrain him. "You gotta listen to management," Star-Man tells him. "Without us you'd be just like a mad dog again [like Kosmo in *The Mad Dog Blues*?]. Can't you remember what that was like." Hoss is further restricted by the code—as a star, he can no longer operate outside it like the Gypsy Markers do—and by his sense of history, of the roots from which his music comes. In addition, he feels old: "I can't do a Lee Marvin in the late sixties," he tells Becky.

In an attempt to build his self-confidence, Hoss sends for Galactic Jack, one of the big disc jockeys. When he shows up with his charts, Hoss gets right down to the big question: "Just give it to me straight. Am I risin' or fallin'." Jack responds that he is a "shootin' star . . . high flyin' and no jivin'," and that the bookies have Hoss at two to one to hit the top. Jack describes the fight for first place in terms of a car race, but assures Hoss that "the course is clear" except for "a few Gypsy Killers comin' into the picture." But it is the Gypsy Killers that Hoss is mostly worried about. They are like the "hot shot young dudes" that Slim in *Back Bog Beast Bait* describes. "They've got time on their side," Hoss argues. "The youth's goin' to 'em. The kids are flocking to Gypsy Kills. It's a market opening up, Jack. I got a feeling. I know they're on their way in and we're going out. We're gettin' old, Jack."

Hoss's success has bred restriction rather than freedom. When he suggests taking a cruise in his Maserati, Becky tells him it is too dangerous. Word has come that one of the Gypsies has marked Hoss; he is a prisoner in his own pad. As a result, he decides to move, to live outside the law, to break the code just as everyone else is doing. He might even take on the Keepers, who run the whole system. To his driver Cheyenne, he makes an elegant plea to return to what they were before success ruined them:

> Can't you see what's happened to us. We ain't Markers no more. We ain't even Rockers. We're punk chumps cowering under the Keepers and the Refs and the critics and the public eye. We ain't free no more! Goddamnit! We ain't flying' in the eye of contempt. We've become respectable and safe. Soft, mushy chewable ass lickers. What's happened to our killer heart. What's happened to our blind fucking courage! Cheyenne, we ain't got much time, man. We were warriors once.

To this plea Cheyenne turns a deaf ear, and the fighting spirit drains out of Hoss. He laments the breakdown of the code, the loss of tradition, the degeneration of the game into street fighting. "Without a code it's just crime," he so-liloquizes. "No art involved. No technique, finesse. No sense of mastery. The touch is gone." From this lament he lapses into sentimentality and nostalgia. He remembers the old West when a young gunfighter named Doc Carter followed William F. Cody around but never was able to get out of his shadow. "I suppose nowadays he'd just take over the whole show," Hoss concludes. When Becky enters bringing Hoss some knives to practice with for his show-down with the Gypsy, Hoss only wants to reminisce: "You remember the El Monte Legion Stadium? . . . Ripple Wine? . . . The Coasters?" He thinks of running away, but Becky tells him there is no place to go, the old world is gone: "The streets are controlled by the packs. . . . The packs are controlled by the gangs. . . . They're controlled by cross syndicates. The next step is the Keepers." Hoss cannot believe what he hears: "What about the country. Ain't there any farmers left, ranchers, cowboys, open space? Nobody just livin' their life." To sooth him Becky sings about the old days of the open road when there were no demands on him, when all he had to do was to "watch the rhythm of the line" and "listen to the song that the V–8 sings."

Cheyenne interrupts this reverie with news that the Gypsy is coming in fast driving a '58 Impala. Hoss begins to get ready; he remembers a time in high school when he and two buddies attacked eight rich kids from Arcadia at Bob's Big Boy. "It was like John Wayne, Robert Mitchum and Kirk Douglas all in one movie." But now he is no longer "a true Marker." With everyone depending on him he has become "a fucking industry." He is tired and has to get some sleep; tomorrow he must fight for his place.

In act 2 Hoss and Crow face each other in a prolonged verbal boxing match. From the very beginning, Crow "ex-udes violent arrogance and cruises the stage with true con-tempt," while Hoss comes on mildly, unable to hide his profound loss of confidence. Crow speaks in a new lan-guage that Hoss finds hard to understand. To Hoss's re-quest to "back the language up" because he is "too old to follow the flash," Crow coolly offers to let Hoss "choose an argot." In response to Crow's jargon and style, Hoss adopts a series of voices and images, and quite naturally he begins with a cowboy line that begins to make Crow nervous because it is out of his range. Not realizing his advantage, Hoss switches at the prodding of Crow, to 1920s gangster style. Crow regains his confidence, but Hoss, thinking he has Crow "down on one knee," goes off to get a referee for the rest of the match. While Hoss is gone, Crow sings a song that reveals one of the reasons for his strength. It begins with an acknowledgment that the same winds that blow for him blow for Hoss and that neither of them knows the law that keeps them both "lost at sea." But Crow has an advantage that we learn later Hoss does not have: "I believe in my mask—The Man I made up is me / And I believe in my dance—And my destiny." Unlike Hoss, who can switch voices because he does not believe that any of them are really his, Crow never switches voices because he believes that the one he projects is not a voice at all but is his true self. He believes in the mask he has created.

With the arrival of the Ref, the showdown begins in earnest. Using microphones, Hoss and Crow fire words at each other "in rhythmic patterns." Crow begins by constructing an adolescent past for Hoss built mainly out of shame and loss: "The first to run. The shame kid. The first on his heel. Shame on the shame kid. Never live it down. Never show his true face. Last in line. Never face a showdown. Never meet a face-off. Never make a clean break. Long line a' losers." Hoss rejects the picture, but Crow does not let up until the round ends, and the Ref declares him the winner.

In round 2 Hoss goes on the offensive by adopting the style of an "ancient delta blues singer." Crow immediately becomes nervous because he is a man without roots, without a musical past. Hoss gives him a quick history of blues, to which Crow responds weakly. "I'm a Rocker, not a hick!" Knowing that he has him running, Hoss continues: "You could use a little cow flop on yer shoes, boy. Yo' music's in yo' head. You a blind minstrel with a phoney shuffle. . . . You doin' a pantomime in the eye of a hurricane. . . . You lost the barrelhouse, you lost the honkey-tonk. . . . You ripped your own self off and now all you got is yo' poison to call yo' gift." Hoss has found Crow's weakness, but the Ref intervenes and calls the round a draw because he "can't make heads or tails outa this" any more than Crow.

Round 3 puts Crow back on the offensive. He attacks Hoss as a man who cannot get it together either musically or sexually: "Can't get it together for all of his tryin'. Can't get it together for fear that he's dyin'. . . . Busted and dyin' and cryin' for more. Busted and bleedin' all over the floor. All bleedin' and wasted and tryin' to score." The violence of the words causes the Ref to step in and declare the match over, giving it to Crow on a technical knockout.

Although Hoss objects at first, he finally admits he is defeated and offers to give up his turf if Crow will teach him how to be a Gypsy. Hoss begins to pick up Crow's style until a new image of himself begins to form: "Mean and tough and cool. Untouchable. A true killer. . . . True to his voice. . . . Beyond doubt. . . . Trusts every action to be what it is. . . . Unending trust in himself. . . . Holds no grudge. No blame. No guilt. . . . Passed beyond tears. Beyond ache for the world. Pitiless. Indifferent and riding in a state of grace." But Hoss is not Crow, and he comes hard up against the very thing that separates the two of them. "It ain't me! IT AIN'T ME! IT AIN'T ME! IT AIN'T ME!" he cries. Hoss is not his image; he sees himself from the outside. For Crow, on the other hand, the image is all there is; it is his "survival kit."

His time, his images, and himself all used up, Hoss makes the only gesture of originality left to him, "a true gesture that won't never cheat on itself 'cause it's the last of its kind." He puts a gun in his mouth and pulls the trigger, leaving Becky, his Maserati, and his place on the charts to Crow.

The Tooth of Crime is the culmination of everything Shepard had been working toward since 1964 and the summation of all his interests and obsessions. It is his most sophisticated and penetrating statement on the role of the artist and the condition of art in contemporary American society, his most developed use of music within the Brechtian model, and his most extensive and intricate use of certain key icons of popular culture. Woven into the thematic fabric of the play are all the motifs most common to his work: the cowboy as an itinerant hero and figure of legend, the relationship between art and commerce, the ineradicable violence in the American psyche, the movies as wellspring of metaphor and cultural models, the essential conflict between father and son (certainly the relationship between Hoss and Crow must be seen in these terms as well as in artistic ones), the perpetual chafing against confinement and the desire to escape, and the road as the only place where real action and freedom are.

In *The Tooth of Crime*, more than in any of his other plays, Sam Shepard gave the theater back to language. Setting, action, plot are all sacrificed to the power of the word, a power that Shepard once said was "like pulling out a .38 when someone faces you with a knife."[12] His language engages the reader and the audience in this way by confronting them with a force greater than the one they bring to it. It is relentless in its richness of association and reference, in its bold use of the jargons of popular culture, in its changes of style, and in its pure inventiveness. The language of the play is both thought and felt; it is at once "pure elegance of intellect"[13] and living incantation capable of evoking "visions in the eye of the audience."[14] It is the substance of one of the great plays of the American theater.

Although *The Tooth of Crime* was originally presented at the Open Space in London, a New York production was soon mounted by the Performance Group under the direction of Richard Schechner. As with many productions of his plays, Shepard was dissatisfied with the staging. "When you write a play," he commented, "it sets up certain assumptions about the context in which it's to be performed, and in that play they had nothing to do with what Schechner set up in the theatre." With few exceptions, this

12. "Language, Visualization, and the Inner Library," p. 217.
13. McClure, "Introduction," p. 2.
14. "Language, Visualization, and the Inner Library," p. 216.

comment might apply to most directors Shepard has worked with. As a result, he found himself taking over the direction of his next play, *Geography of a Horse Dreamer*, an experience which he said opened his "eyes to all possibilities of productions."[15]

Although he had played for very high stakes and had won with *The Tooth of Crime*, Shepard modified his aims in *Geography of a Horse Dreamer*. Using simpler language, drawn as he has said from Raymond Chandler and Dashiell Hammett, he created his own version of a thirties-style crime drama, though not without a guest appearance by two cowboys. In addition to honing down his language, Shepard also narrowed the play thematically, concentrating on the problem of the artist as a prisoner to commercial needs, always under the pressure to perform. Throughout the play, Cody (his name taken significantly from a Western hero) is referred to by such names as Mr. Artistic Cowboy, Beethoven, and plain Mr. Artistic. He is a dreamer who for a time loses his ability to dream, who complains that those feeding off him don't understand "the space inside where the dream comes," and who is finally rescued from confinement by an image of the old West.

The play's metaphor for artistic production is Cody's ability to pick the winners of horse races, an ability which is being used by a criminal element that holds Cody a perpetual prisoner. Act 1, subtitled "The Slump," opens in "an old sleazy hotel room." Cody, dressed in western style, is tied to a bed and guarded by Santee and Beaujo, both wearing movie-gangster clothing. Under orders from Fingers, they have kidnapped Cody from Wyoming and have been using him to pick winners for them. He is in a slump, however, and they have been forced to move from posh surroundings at the Beverly Wilshire to a cheap hotel in England. There they wait for Cody to get back into stride again, though recently he has given them only horses from the past while his real dreams are about the Great Plains. He complains about being "dried up" and needing "a break" and about not knowing what country he is being

15. Chubb, "Metaphors," pp. 203–4.

held in. "It's stupid!" he exclaims. "It's really stupid! I'm dreaming American horses and we're probably in Morocco somewhere. . . . I gotta know where we are so's I can adjust." Cody's argument links him to his creator and recalls a comment Shepard once made about the relationship between writing and environment:

> I have a feeling that the cultural environment one is raised in predetermines a rhythmical relationship to the use of words. In this sense, I can't be anything other than an American writer. . . . After living in England for three straight years, . . . certain subtle changes occurred in this rhythmic construction. In order to accommodate these new configurations . . . , I found myself adding English characters to my plays. *Geography of a Horse Dreamer* was written in London, and there's only one truly American character in the play.[16]

Getting no satisfaction on any of his complaints or questions, Cody asks for some sleeping pills, and while he is drifting off recapitulates with Beaujo how long this business has been going on and how it got started. Their recounting of events is a brief précis of the commercializing of an artist, indicating that Cody was as much seduced as he was kidnapped: the first big dream; publicity; *Life* magazine; the exploitation of his ability by his parents, brothers, and "half the state of Wyoming"; and finally the temptation of being "wined and dined" by Fingers and his gang.

Disgusted by the lack of results from Cody, Santee calls Fingers to find out what to do and is directed to try dog racing. Santee is humiliated by this change, but Cody begins picking dog winners immediately, becoming an instant expert on the entire subject. Like Shepard, who also became interested in dog racing while in England, Cody is simply accommodating the "new configurations" of a new environment, even to the point of adopting an Irish accent when making his pronouncements.

Act 2, subtitled "The Hump," finds the fortunes of Cody and his exploiters much improved. They are rich again and live in a fancy hotel. Cody is still speaking in an Irish accent

16. "Language, Visualization, and the Inner Library," p. 216.

and giving advice on dog racing. Unexpectedly, Fingers and the doctor arrive, causing a fearful reaction in Cody, who retreats to the other side of the room. As Cody becomes more and more like a frightened dog, Fingers begins to feel guilty for the "terrible sin" he has committed in keeping Cody a prisoner, and he decides to let him go, to return him to Wyoming. But the doctor, whom Shepard describes as looking like Sydney Greenstreet, suddenly takes over. He tells the others that in the neck of every dreamer is a magical bone that "collects certain valuable substances from his dreams." Possessing these bones endows the owner with some of the magic of the dreamer. The doctor has been collecting these bones and proposes to remove the one from Cody's neck. Cody tries to deny his power, but the doctor tells him it is even greater than he thinks: "If he knew his power he could even make us disappear. Fortunately he's just a slave for us." This remark has a double meaning. First, it is another statement about the power of the artist to free himself; he does not have to participate in his own seduction. Second, since Cody can be seen to represent the artist and therefore Shepard himself, and since the play is an act of the imagination, the work of a dreamer, all the characters are a product of the artist's conception; they are not a reality or a necessity and can be changed or eliminated by the author. And, in fact, they are, by Shepard's sudden introduction of Cody's two brothers, Jasper and Jason, who burst into the room and rescue Cody by killing the doctor, Santee, and Beaujo. That they are dressed in authentic western style is further indication that they function as direct expressions of the author's imagination and will.

Geography of a Horse Dreamer testifies to an apparent resolution of some of the confusions and constraints expressed in *The Mad Dog Blues, Cowboy Mouth, Back Bog Beast Bait,* and *The Tooth of Crime.* Although Cody has to be rescued by forces outside himself, and therefore seems incapable of achieving his own freedom, the obvious artificiality and theatricality of the means used to rescue him, and the sudden willfulness with which they appear, reveal the power and freedom of the author, of Shepard himself. His ability to create characters and action in his art becomes a metaphor for his ability to shape his own life. If commercialization is more a seduction than a kidnapping, as the play implies, the artist need only be made of sterner stuff in order to free himself. This message exists in the earlier plays as well, but its restatement in *Geography of a Horse Dreamer* seems less hedged by doubts and therefore more definite and capable of practical application.

Shepard's last play to be written and staged in England was *Action*. It has been compared to the European theater of the absurd, and in some ways it suggests the influence of Samuel Beckett. Contrary to its title, its four characters are incapable of any significant action. The actions they do perform are basically devoid of meaning, so they try to give them meaning by the way in which they talk about them. They are isolated, alienated human beings who do things without reference to each other, who live in enclosed spaces, both physically and psychologically, and who cannot bridge the gap between their private selves and their social selves. The difference between what they are and what they think they are, between being and seeming, produces a condition of estrangement that at first seems strange itself because we are so used to hiding our own estrangement from others. Shepard pinpointed this problem in a poem he included in *Motel Chronicles*:

> Why am I thinking
> "This guy is totally crazy"
> Sitting in a country cafe
> Dressed in a black velvet three-piece suit
> Smelling like a 14th Street Pimp
> Horizontally twitching brown eyes
> With no pupil to speak of
>
> Why am I thinking
> "This guy is a maniac"
> When he asks if it's ever snowed in San Francisco
> If Herb Alpert plays classical music
>
> Why am I thinking
> "This man is nuts"
> When he tells me he's a man of many talents
> But he doesn't have time to develop any one of them

112

Why am I thinking
"This guy is bananas"
When he picks up the cream pitcher
And calls it a "Cute Cow"

I know why it is
It's because he's not concealing
His desperate estrangement from people

This basic human problem is highlighted by three stories that are told during the course of the play. The first one, related by Shooter, is about a man who felt separate from his body, until one day his body rebelled and killed him and then went off on its own. Jeep and Shooter speculate on whether they could tell that the body was vacant if they happened to encounter it. The second story, also told by Shooter, is about moths seeking to understand the flame of a candle that they see glowing in the window of a house. Two moths fly close, but only the third one, which flies right into the flame and unites with it, really understands it. Jeep tells the third story, an account of himself in jail, where he had the desperate thought that he could not escape and that the walls were closing in on him.

The same elements that can be talked about from this psychological and social standpoint raise formal questions as well. The most important is the relationship between character and action. From the beginning, Shepard had rejected traditional notions of character in favor of figures lacking the precise definition as psychological and social entities. This makes for characters who do not encourage audience identification but rather function as flexible mouthpieces for the author. It also necessitates separating action from character and ascribing its motivation to the author directly. The audience's sense of character, therefore, comes less from mimesis than it does from the language itself and from the signifying aspects of gesture, props, setting, lighting, and music. From this perspective *Action* finds its source in Brecht more than Beckett and, in terms of Shepard's total body of work, most directly parallels his 1966 play *Fourteen Hundred Thousand*.

Action is constructed out of precise and repeating gestures. The four characters, two men and two women, all in their late twenties or early thirties, spend much of the time around a simple board table in the downstage area. They sip coffee in unison, take turns trying to find the place where they left off in a book they are reading, stare at each other blankly even during conversation, and generally do not react to the events going on around them. When Jeep twice loses control and each time smashes a chair to pieces, the others show no sense of surprise: "They look at the chair together as though seeing it as an event outside themselves."

This distance between the characters and the actions shortcircuits one of the principal ways in which characters relate to each other. If they cannot connect to the events, they cannot connect to each other through the events. If, in addition, their gestures are made mechanical and automatic and they confront each other with blank stares, then only language remains to bridge the gap. Separating language from action, or having language and action operate on separate levels, distances the audience's emotions and allows language to dominate.

In 1977 Shepard assigned *Action* a special place among his plays as the one that had most resolved a basic theatrical problem. "I began to see," he wrote, "that the living outcome (the production) always demanded a different kind of attention than the written form that it sprang from. The spoken word, no matter how you cut it, is different than the written word. It happens in a different space, under different circumstances and demands a different set of laws. *Action* . . . comes the closest to sounding on stage exactly like it was written." [17] He ascribed this result to having spoken "each line out loud" before writing it down, but his conscious concern with the relationships among character, action, and language and his separation of these elements through a highly formal technique also seems to have played a large part in preserving the original written form of the language in its spoken expression.

17. Ibid., p. 218.

Late in 1974 Shepard and his family returned to the United States and settled in the San Francisco Bay area. Productions of *Action* opened at the American Place Theatre in New York and the Magic Theatre in San Francisco. It won for Shepard his second Obie award for distinguished play. He also wrote a short theatrical monologue called *Killer's Head*, which was first presented at the American Place Theatre in 1975 and acted by Richard Gere. Played on a bare stage with the character, Mazon, strapped to an electric chair, the monologue works from a contradiction between the situation and what Mazon talks about. The time setting is the few minutes before Mazon's electrocution, but the content of the monologue is entirely trivial, as if Mazon had all the time in the world. He talks about buying a truck and breeding horses, in a way that completely ignores what is about to happen to him. "Oh yeah, today's the day I buy the pick-up," he begins. Three-fourths of the way through the monologue he pauses for a full minute before continuing, as if to emphasize his utter contempt for the proceedings at hand. The piece ends with his electrocution in darkness, his body lighting up momentarily before everything fades to black.

Before getting back into his theatrical stride in 1976, when he produced three major plays, Shepard signed on with Bob Dylan's Rolling Thunder Revue in order to write dialogue for a film to be made while the group was on tour. Plans for the film were rather vague, but Shepard was to go along and fit somehow into the improvisatory nature of the project. The film went progressively to pieces as the Revue traveled through the Northeast. On Thanksgiving Day 1975 at a Holiday Inn in Maine, Shepard left the tour and returned to New York, catching up to it again on 9 December at Madison Square Garden for the Revue's final concert. Although the film was scrapped, Shepard published an account of the experience under the title *Rolling Thunder Logbook*.

With the Rolling Thunder Revue, England, and New York behind him, Shepard settled into California. Also behind him were several experiences with the movies, the most prominent of which was his association with Michelangelo Antonioni on *Zabriskie Point*. His work on the screenplay for that film had brought him into intimate contact with the money, power, glitter, and essential corruption of Hollywood. For his first major work since *Action* he chose Hollywood as his subject, and on 2 July 1976 *Angel City* opened at the Magic Theatre under Shepard's own direction.

Although he has expressed interest in writing and directing a film and has built a successful career as a film actor, Shepard has long been wary of the movie industry and scornful of Hollywood people. "They ooze and call each other 'darlings,'" he wrote in *Motel Chronicles*. "They hire fortune tellers who lie . . . / their loneliness is covered with grins / their loneliness is smothered in a circle of 'friends.'" *Angel City* is a biting satire on Hollywood and the writer who goes there with disdain on his lips but lust for power in his heart.

Once again Shepard uses a bare stage, with only a few significant props: a blue neon rectangle suspended in the center of the upstage area, which represents a movie screen; a large swivel chair, a seat for those in power; a hand-held microphone, used to lend authority to narration sequences; and two tympani drums, which often provide musical commentary on the action. The chair is placed so that it faces the rectangle, though it can also swivel to face the audience. Behind the rectangle covering the upstage wall is a scrim, which can be lit with different colors.

As the play opens, Tympani begins a roll on his drums that rises to high pitch and intensity before it suddenly stops. This theatrical device is used as a tongue-in-cheek introduction of Lanx, a stereotypical Hollywood producer, who is seated unseen in the swivel chair, his back to the audience. Speaking over the microphone, Lanx delivers a narration about the city as seen through his window. Since he is facing the rectangle, the window functions as a conventional metaphor for the screen, and his description is understood in terms of classical Hollywood cinema: "It's a great window. A great life. All hell passes before me, and I can watch it like a junkie. With no pain." From this addictive yet totally vicarious perspective, Lanx gives a hyperbolic and conventionally surreal picture of Los Angeles:

> The city teems with living things. Things crawl across upholstered seats. Deals are made in glove compartments. And we exist, here, walled in. A booming industry. . . . Grossing fifty million in just two weeks. . . . Outside, the smog strikes clean to the heart. . . . Used-car lots melt away into the black macadam. . . . And all along through the terrifying shopping centers the doom merchants whisper our fate.

As Lanx is beginning his narration, Rabbit enters. "Dressed in a tattered detective's type suit" and carrying Indian medicine bundles attached to him by leather thongs, he seems very much out of place. He has just arrived by buckboard from the North. Like Shepard, Rabbit does not fly, so it has taken him a long time to get to Angel City. He has also stopped off at all the missions along his route in order to pray. Without introducing himself or giving any information, Lanx asks Rabbit what he thinks of the narration. "Terrible," he replies. "Old time. Worse than Jack Webb I'd say." Lanx agrees and outlines his problem and the reason why he and his partner Wheeler have asked Rabbit to come. They have gotten themselves into a project that is in deep trouble, and they need someone to get them out. They have called on Rabbit because he is not just a scriptwriter but an artist, or according to Lanx, "a kind of magician or something." Like Cody in *Geography of a Horse Dreamer*, he can "dream things up." What Lanx wants is "something awesome and totally new." When Rabbit asks if they have tried holographs, Lanx replies, "No, no! You don't get the picture. We're looking for an actual miracle. Nothing technological. The real thing."

Left alone for a while, Rabbit confesses to the audience his real motives for coming:

> The point is I've smelled something down here. Something sending its sweet claws way up North. . . . Causing me wonder at the life of a recluse. The vision of a celluloid tape with a series of moving images telling a story to millions. . . . Effecting [sic] their dreams and actions. Replacing their books. Replacing their families. Replacing religion, politics, art, con-

versation. Replacing their minds. . . . So I wind up here, in the city of the South. Not knowing a thing but convincing them through mysterious gestures that I'm their main man. I'm ravenous for power but I have to conceal it.

The second half of this confession is accompanied by the "slow and mournful" music of a saxophone player who stands behind the neon rectangle. In contrast to the tympani music, the sax is a sound connected to the past and to real meaning and feeling. When Lanx returns and finds the saxophone player on stage, he chases him off because of his association with the past. "GET OUTA' HERE YOU CREEP!" shouts Lanx. "Continuously trying to reverberate us into the past with that solo crap."

Although he first adopts a sheepish stance, Wheeler turns out to be the real power, the "genius producer," who is actually a fearful and uncreative man. His biggest problem, however, which he blames on the city, is that he is turning into a reptile of some kind. "The city is eating us alive," he tells Rabbit. "Can't you see my skin? Look at my skin." His desperation is greater than Lanx's, and consequently he is more precise as to what their real desire is: "Not simply an act of terror but something which will in fact drive people right off the deep end. . . . Create mass hypnosis. Suicide. Auto-destruction. Something which will open entirely new fads in sado-masochism. . . . That's what the people are crying out for and that's what we must give them. . . . We owe it to the public."

This wonderful parody of the old cliche of the Hollywood producer—"We are only giving the public what it wants"—takes Rabbit aback: "Now hold on a second, man. This sounds like something totally out of my ball park. . . . I'm a stunt man. I fall off horses. I've done some sleight of hand. I've conjured a little bit. I collect a few myths, but this sounds like you need a chemical expert or something." Wheeler is not about to let Rabbit turn back, however, and he gives him until the end of the week to come up with something.

Rabbit soon finds out from Tympani that there is no getting away (the confinement/escape theme so common in Shepard's work). "They'll swallow you whole and spit you

118

out as a tax deduction," Tympani tells him. He learns that Tympani, also, is working on something similar, though from a musical angle, trying to discover a rhythm that will produce "trance states in masses of people." Rabbit enlists the aid of Tympani and of Miss Scoons, an ambitious studio secretary, to help him solve his problem. Both are problematic allies, however, since Tympani accepts his servitude as inescapable and Miss Scoons does not think she is in servitude. In addition, Miss Scoons is a prisoner of the movies in a way that is quite common. After agreeing to help Rabbit, she becomes momentarily entranced by the rectangle and begins speaking in a monotone: "I look at the screen and I am the screen. . . . I look at the movie and I am the movie. . . . I am the star in the movie. For days I am the star and I'm not me. I'm me being the star. I look at my life when I come down. I look and I hate my life when I come down. I hate my life not being a movie. I hate my life not being a star. I hate being myself in my life which isn't a movie and never will be."

In *Motel Chronicles*, Shepard writes of a similar experience from reality. On the last day of location shooting of a film he was acting in, he encountered the stand-in for the star. She was stoned on Valium and white wine and was deeply depressed because she would have to stay behind in her hometown while the movie crew would be moving on. Like Miss Scoons, she hated her life because it did not measure up to the movie. "And it made me suddenly re-ashamed of being an actor in a movie at all," he wrote, "and provoking such stupid illusions." In desperation she even tried to throw herself out a window. When Shepard tried to comfort her by saying it was "just a dumb movie" and was not worth being depressed about, she replied with a line worthy of *Angel City*: "It's not as dumb as life."[18] It is this dream aspect of the movies, which sometimes causes people to hate their own lives, that seems to define for Shepard the ultimate problem of movies in American life.

As act 1 moves toward conclusion, things become more

18. *Motel Chronicles*, p. 41.

frantic. Rabbit, Tympani, and Miss Scoons have not found any solution to the problem, movie thinking rather than reality thinking is coming to dominate even Rabbit's consciousness, and Lanx returns in desperation because Wheeler is getting worse. He has turned green and his skin is beginning to peel. Rabbit complains that he cannot work in this environment because he is an artist, but Lanx and Tympani make it quite clear that Rabbit was drawn there by his desire for money. Meanwhile, Miss Scoons, in a trancelike state, begins having apocalyptic visions about ambition and greed as devouring forces. Lanx feels that they will all be eaten alive. Each character progressively slips into his world of preoccupations and obsessions until Wheeler rushes on, his skin all green and his face and arms covered with sores, and shouts, "WHERE'S MY DISASTER!!!!!!!!!!!!!!!!!"

As act 2 begins, Wheeler has gotten worse (he has slimy skin, long fingernails, and fangs), and Rabbit finally gets to work with his Indian medicine bundles. He explains to Wheeler, who now occupies the swivel chair, that there is one bundle for each of the four major points of the compass. Only the bundle for the west, however, is truly powerful. The west is the "Looks-Within" place, the place of looking within the self. It is dangerous because of the unknown things that can be found there. On the bundle for the west is a warning that should it be opened, "a terrible force will be let loose in the world."

As he works and argues with Wheeler, Rabbit suddenly sees that there is no problem to solve because Wheeler does not in fact have a movie; he only has a disaster, which is himself. Wheeler's response, though meant to counter Rabbit's charge, actually validates it and explains the physical condition from which Wheeler is suffering. "I HAVE A MILLION MOVIES!" he shouts. "AND DO YOU KNOW WHERE THEY ARE! THEY'RE IN MY BLOOD! . . . EVERY ONE OF THEM IS TEARING ME APART! . . . TRYING TO OOZE OUT AND TAKE ON A SHAPE THAT WE ALL CAN SEE! AND EVERY ONE OF THEM IS EATING ME! CHEWING ME APART FROM THE INSIDE OUT! A MILLION DEVILS!" It is the movies themselves that are turning Wheeler into a monster. "I was turned into this beyond my knowing," he tells Rabbit. "I was spawned somehow by a city. I was leaked out. . . . Monsters are being hatched by the dozens and turned into saints! We can do anything here! . . . We can recreate the world and make you swallow it whole!" He confronts Rabbit with the claim that the two of them are the same, for what they fear makes them equal.

Finally, Wheeler forces Rabbit into the swivel chair to watch the rushes of the movie he has been making. The neon rectangle lights up, and Wheeler narrates a story about two generals who fought a battle that took them beyond time and history, only to discover that one of them was a woman and that they were part of the same being. While Wheeler speaks, Lanx and Miss Scoons act out a samurai battle, dressed in crash helmets and football padding. At the end of the story, Rabbit declares it the corniest stuff he has ever seen. When Wheeler swivels the chair around, demanding to know what is wrong with it, Rabbit is revealed as a monster, too. He has the same slimy green skin, fangs, and long fingernails that Wheeler has, and he declares, as if he were Wheeler, "There's no disaster! We're not interested in hankey pankey love stories, romantically depicting the end of the world. We're after hard core disaster." With the two monsters now facing each other, Rabbit tells Wheeler, "You might as well burn that footage up. . . . You're washed up in this town, buddy." In response, Wheeler opens the medicine bundle for the west, and a stream of green liquid begins oozing out over the stage.

Throughout this final confrontation between Wheeler and Rabbit, Lanx and Miss Scoons have been watching them "as though in the movies." Speaking as if she were a teenage girl on a date, Miss Scoons says, "I'm not supposed to stay for the second one ya' know Jimmy." In effect, the play ends as it began. It opened with Lanx narrating a movie, and it ends with the play itself treated as a movie— but only for the characters. Despite the hilarity of its ironic treatment, it must be Shepard's hope that the audience's viewing experience is not, as Lanx said about the movie experience, without pain. The play's intention is to un-mask both the Hollywood system and the kind of illusion-istic and fundamentally deceiving films that encourage people to hate their own lives. At the same time, he paro-dies the often self-justifying pose of the artist who tries to disguise his attraction to the money, glamour, and power of the movie industry as an attempt to upgrade its artistic quality. As he did in *Geography of a Horse Dreamer*, Shepard calls for a recognition of the artist's complicity in his own seduction.

Also in 1976, the Yale Repertory Theatre produced *Sui-cide in B♭*, a play in which Shepard tried to put to rest some of the ghosts that had been haunting him for a long time. While still in England, he confided to an interviewer, "I'd like to try a whole different way of writing now, which is very stark and not so flashy and not full of a lot of mythic figures."[19] The flash and the myths had served Shepard well, however, and dropping them would not be easy. To aid in the process, Shepard chose to do what other artists before and after him have done; he made some of his men-tal wrestlings public. *Suicide in B♭* airs the issue of breaking with the past and, in the process, raises many basic ques-tions regarding the role of the artist that are found throughout Shepard's work.

Appropriate to the play's theatrical subject, Shepard specifies a stage set that calls attention to itself as a set. A white muslim flat is used as the upstage wall. "It should be made obvious that it's a flat to the audience," states Shepard in the scene directions. In addition, the flat does not extend the full width of the stage, there are no walls on the sides, and the floor is left bare. Only a few essential props are used to articulate this open space: a piano against the upstage flat, a stuffed chair downstage left, and a brass floor lamp next to the chair.

Shepard has subtitled the play *A Mysterious Overture*, suggesting both its crime-melodrama plot and its musical associations. The action revolves around a crime that may or may not have occurred and the attempts of two comi-

19. Chubb, "Metaphors," p. 208.

cally developed detectives, Pablo and Louis, to sort out the evidence and solve the mystery. Niles, the assumed victim, was a poor jazz musician, though, as it turns out, he is not dead but in hiding. Who then was the corpse found in Niles's apartment with his face blown off? And who killed him? Pablo and Louis arrest Niles at the end of the play but the correctness of this action can only be explained on a level other than the plot.

Shepard loses no time in establishing this other level. The first line encapsulates the play's most important meaning: "Trying to re-construct the imagination of it." On the immediate level, this comment refers to the attempt by Pablo and Louis to reconstruct the crime, but the peculiar wording of the statement implies much more. The line does not say that they are trying to reconstruct the crime (*it*), but instead the *imagination* of it. "The imagination," repeats Pablo. "The imagination of it. How we suppose it might have been." Since they were not witnesses to the crime, they can only imagine what it was, and therefore they are not really restaging the crime, but only staging their imaginative concept of the crime. In a similar way, the staging of the play is a reconstruction of the imagination of the playwright. From this perspective, Pablo and Louis are more than detectives looking for evidence; they are characters in search of an author. Near the end of the play, it becomes abundantly clear that all the characters are involved in this search; Laureen and Petrone, two young musicians who have been waiting for Niles, finally confront him:

> Niles: What's happened to all of you?
> Laureen: We've been waiting.
> Niles: For me?
> Laureen: We've been waiting to play.

Niles, however, is reluctant to take on the responsibility that this role entails, and to Laureen he replies, "You don't need me for that." Like Slim in *Cowboy Mouth*, he tries to escape the part being thrust upon him.

Despite his resistance, Niles can no more avoid responsibility than can Shepard, and in fact, Shepard uses Niles

123

to voice his own artistic conflicts, thereby making the character an extension of the author. He even endows him with a childhood that corresponds to his own. Niles tells Paulette, a young girl who is helping him, about growing up on an island, and the experience he recounts is identical to Shepard's description of the time he spent on Guam: being in the house made of tin and hearing the sound of rain on the roof; the Japanese soldiers emerging from the jungle at night to steal laundry off the lines; his mother keeping a .45 automatic pistol next to her in case the Japanese do come; and going to see *Song of the South* at a drive-in.

To help set the stage for the first appearance of Niles and his discussions of the artistic fix he finds himself in, Louis presents a theory about Niles's disappearance that is actually not a theory at all but a discourse on the nature of art and a biographical sketch that strongly resembles events in Shepard's life. It begins with the artist in a prenatal state, already hearing sounds, "gurgling, pounding under water . . . an ocean of blood swimming around him." He is born and discovers that he has a voice, that he can hear himself grow, that the world around him is made up of sounds. "Then one day he hears what they call music. . . . Music as an extension of sound. An organization. Another way of putting it." This other way of perceiving the world is art, an imaginative organization of what in its raw form is just noise. This discovery marks the birth of the artist, who is different from other people. "He has a revelation. Or rather, a revelation presents itself. . . . Enters into him and becomes part of his physiology. . . . He puts it to use. He's driven toward it in a way most men consider dangerous and suicidal." At this point Louis's monologue, though it continues to describe a general condition, begins to incorporate elements that are biographically and artistically related to Shepard. The artist of Louis's theory becomes enormously prolific, boldly experimental, and world famous, as Shepard had done. "Then one day he disappears. . . . Rumors are spread that he's kidnapped. . . . Talk of him being involved with particular ladies." If we take *Cowboy Mouth* as a guide, this evokes Shepard's relationship with Patti Smith and further suggests his flight to

England shortly after, a reference that is reinforced by Petrone when he remarks that Niles has gone out to get English muffins.

Pablo also raises the question of art during his interrogation of Petrone: "What do you know about improvisation?" When Petrone refuses to answer, Pablo launches into a diatribe against new artistic forms that could just as well have been directed at Shepard: "How does it relate to breaking with tradition! To breaking off with the past! To throwing the diligent efforts of our forefathers and their forefathers before them to the winds! To turning the classics to garbage before our very eyes! To distorting the very foundations of our cherished values! . . . To rubbing up against the very grain of sanity and driving us all to complete and utter destruction!" To emphasize the hysteria behind this kind of attack, the piano breaks in and accompanies it "with loud atonal chords" played "at random intervals."

To pacify Pablo, Petrone begins telling the life story of Niles. While this is occurring, Niles and Paullette enter, and although the two different groups occupy the same space, they take no cognizance of each other. Niles has returned to the scene of the crime to make a break with the past by killing the mythic figures who have been central to his art but who also are causing him to repeat himself. Appropriately, given his relation to Shepard, Niles begins with the Western hero. "I hate killing this one first," he tells Paulette, and, as if to reassure himself that the myths are independent of his own use of them, he sings, "Pecos Bill, Pecos Bill / Never died / And he never will / Oh, Pecos Bill." He pleads to leave this figure until last, telling Paullette, "But there's no guarantee I won't die along with him." Paullette responds, "I guarantee it," but Niles is not convinced: "But you don't know how attached I am. I feel as though his skin is my skin." Finally, Paullette pushes the matter by preparing to destroy this mythic figure by shooting an arrow into Niles, who is ritualistically dressed in a cowboy outfit. Niles continues to put off the moment, however, by running through a liturgy of the cowboy's significance: "He's a hero, Paullette! He discovered a whole way of life. . . . Towns sprang up wherever he stopped to wet his whistle. . . . He sang songs to the Milky Way." Paullette counters this mythic description with reality, though in the final analysis only the myth is important: "He's no hero! He's a weasel! He's a punk psychopath built into a big deal by crumby New England rags." As Niles turns his back to receive Paullette's arrow, he constructs an image from the period in which changing times were progressively making the cowboy irrelevant: "It's a bright day. The kind of day you'd never expect to die in. He's got one foot up on the brass rail. . . . Newspapers are printing the news. . . . Scaffolds are being constructed. He sees the nation being built in every small activity. . . . Nothing looks like it could ever die. He doesn't see it coming. He never knew what hit him."

The arrow that strikes Niles also strikes Louis, identifying Louis with the myth of the cowboy and suggesting that he is to be thought of as a figure of Niles's consciousness. On the biographical level, this connection implies that Shepard is not only striking at the restrictions of a particular cultural myth but also at other restrictions of the past, including those represented by his father, since he has given Louis characteristics drawn directly from his father. In distinguishing his own musical tastes from those of Niles, Louis says, "I'm used to Tommy Dorsey, the Mills Brothers, Benny Goodman," the very musicians whose records were listened to in Shepard's childhood home. Louis also talks about his war experiences and refers to scars from wounds that Samuel Shepard Rogers also had.

Having pierced the cowboy image, Niles takes off the costume, puts on black tails, and begins puffing on a cigar. He wonders how this ritualistic acting out can change anything and whether these others that he has to get rid of are just made up by him, just extensions of himself. Paullette tells him that it does not matter because "it's the same." Suddenly, Niles realizes that the one who had his face blown off was really a version of himself. He demands of Paullette, "WHOSE FACE DID WE BLOW OFF?" Her response, "Somebody else's," is a weak denial of Niles's fear that he is indeed giving up some of his own skin when he gives up the images he has believed in. Niles is simultaneously a suicide and a murderer.

At the height of Niles's agitation over this problem, Paulette shoots him, and although it has no apparent effect on him, Pablo begins staggering around the stage as if hit in the stomach. Pablo, too, is an extension of Niles's consciousness, as for that matter are all the other characters. This idea is made clear by Petrone when, speaking metaphorically, he tells Niles, "They're crawling all over your furniture, across your floor, inside your walls." Back in his own house, Niles asks the others a series of questions from which he draws his own conclusion: "What's everyone waiting for? . . . Are you inside me or outside me? Am I inside you? . . . Or am I just like you? . . . So exactly like you that we're exactly the same. So exactly that we're not even apart. Not even separate. Not even two things but just one. Only one."

Niles's insight resolves the mystery on the play's thematic level. In arresting Niles, Louis and Pablo are indeed correct, although they have uncovered more than a simple murderer. As Niles himself makes clear, the detectives have also found their author, the only one who has the right to commit the crime in the first place because he is its ultimate victim. Nevertheless, a crime has been committed and, as Niles points out, "Someone should pay for that." The punishment is the anguish involved in artistic change and in the search for new beginnings that every serious artist, Shepard included, must suffer.

Despite Shepard's expressed desire to move away from mythic figures in his plays and the eloquent treatment of the problematic nature of this desire in *Suicide in Bb*, he gave the mythic one last fling in his ballad play *The Sad Lament of Pecos Bill on the Eve of Killing His Wife*. First performed at the Bay Area Playwright's Festival on 22 October 1976, it seems to take its cue from the ballad refrain that Niles sings about Pecos Bill and from the remark he makes to Paullette that "you can't kill a myth." Through a series of songs, Shepard explores the place of legend in the modern world, sadly concluding that there does not appear to be a place for it. "Why is we both dyin / On this land," sing

Bill and his wife Slue-Foot Sue. "Why is we forsaken / Lost and shamed, forgotten / Why is we both rotten / In the memories of man." Can a myth be killed? Perhaps not, but it can slowly vanish until, as Bill laments, "My legend and time and my myth is forgot."

In his 1978 play *Seduced*, Shepard deals with another kind of legend, that of the man who invents himself. Possible only in the age of mass media, this self-invention is the result of manipulation of an image from a position of great power. Unlike powerful men of the past, however, the play's protagonist, Henry Hackamore, a figure obviously based on Howard Hughes, prefers images to acts and appearances to actualities. As the play opens, he is living in seclusion somewhere in Mexico. He moves only at night; at all other times he remains indoors with the drapes drawn. An old man with long white hair and twisted fingernails, looking like "a cross between a prisoner of war and an Indian fakir," he desires to be an invisible presence, a man without any real contact or feeling, a ghost. His orders are communicated through Raul, whom Henry thinks is his servant, but who in reality is his master. As Henry learns at the end of the play, even his control is just an image, despite the power he once had and believes he still has. At the same time, Henry has a significance that Raul cannot control, a function in American culture revealing that he already is an invisible national presence.

On another level, Henry's desire to manipulate and his preference for images make him into an artist figure, though one who is cut off from areas of experience essential to the artist, or at least to Shepard's conception of the artist. Henry is first seen trying to get Raul to move a potted palm to a different position, though he cannot communicate what he wants him to do with it. "Descriptions don't describe the picture I have in my head," he tells Raul. Finally, frustrated in this attempted bit of stage direction, Henry, who can barely move on his own, asks Raul to rock him back and forth. This movement brings on a flood of images Henry cannot account for. Later, when two women from his past arrive, he directs their telling of a story about

Las Vegas. Like the theater or film director, he moves the two women to their proper positions and instructs them: "Now when you tell this . . . I want you to get real animated. Almost like uh—almost like you were in a movie." When Miami, who begins the story, balks at telling it, Henry asks the other woman, Luna, to take over. To Luna's objection, "But that's her story," Henry gives a specific aesthetic response: "What difference does it make? It's a good story. One story's as good as another. It's all in the way you tell it. That's what counts. That's what makes the difference." Henry's preference, however, is for a conventional telling, and to his great distress Luna moves her story too quickly from one place to another. "No, no, no!!" he shouts. "It doesn't make sense! It's too confusing. . . . What the hell's goin' on here!"

Losing control of the story, Henry begins to feel he is losing control of everything. "Who in the hell's making the decisions around here anyway!" he demands of Raul. He thinks he feels an earthquake, wonders if someone is watching him, has a premonition that the country is being evacuated, and fears a tidal wave is going to wash over them. "Nevada's the only safe ground," he tells Raul. "Only Nevada. I have inside information. Tribal information." Dressing in World War I flying jacket, helmet, and goggles, Henry prepares to return in secret to Las Vegas. He warns Raul against this "evil time" and describes to him the vision of America that has been part of him since boyhood, a vision of total alienation:

> I saw myself. Alone. Standing in open country. Flat, barren. Wasted. . . . Enormous country. Primitive. Screaming with hostility toward men. . . . Toward me. . . . As though men were a joke in the face of it. . . . Miles of heat and wind and red rock where nothing grew but the sand. And far off, invisible little men were huddled against it in cities. . . . I saw the whole world of men as pathetic. Sad, demented little morons moving in circles. . . . Always away from the truth. Getting smaller and smaller until they finally disappeared.

Henry's setting himself apart from all those who are moving away from the truth is brought up short when Raul confronts him with a truth of his own, that all the time

Henry has thought he was in control, he was being manipulated. "I can do anything," Raul tells him. "Anything. I can fabricate any story. Make up any life. Have you disappear in London. Reappear in Brazil. . . . Your life you left to us. To me. I shaped it for you. . . . You can't make a move without me." His power of mise-en-scène out in the open, Raul forces Henry to sign over all his holdings, an action strikingly carried out with a blood-spurting intravenous needle that Raul rips out of Henry's arm. While signing, however, Henry has a sudden insight that carries him beyond the grasp of Raul's simple greed for power: "I see how I disappeared. It happened a long time ago. . . . I disappeared in a dream. I dreamed myself into another shape. . . . I made myself up. . . . I was taken by the dream and all the time I thought I was taking it. It was a sudden seduction. . . . Almost like rape. . . . I gave myself up. Sold it all down the river." This realization in essence turns Henry into an idea. "I'm everywhere!" he tells Raul. "All at once I'm everywhere! I'm all over the country. . . . I'm high over the desert! Invisible. A ghost in the land. . . . A phantom they'll never get rid of. . . . I'm the demon they invented! Everything they ever aspired to. The nightmare of the nation!" Raul begins firing at Henry, but he can't kill him. The man who had turned himself into a legend of hidden power and manipulation, originally raped by a dream but now himself become a rapist, a user and exploiter of the nation, had finally been transformed into the nightmare of the national consciousness, the end product of an aspiration for power and success, the ultimate American.

The years 1970–1976 were crucial ones in Shepard's development as a writer. They began with the recognition of his importance conferred by New York's prestigious Lincoln Center in the Vivian Beaumont production of *Operation Sidewinder*, his most ambitious play to that point. The critical and popular failure of that production returned Shepard to his roots in the Off Off Broadway theater and marked the beginning of a period of reevaluation in which his plays reflected both his personal struggles and the social unrest of the time. *The Mad Dog Blues* and *Cowboy*

Mouth, in particular, define this period in Shepard's work and reveal the conflicts that led to his four years of self-imposed exile in England. Away from America and its contradictions, Shepard gained the distance from his culture that helped define his own place in it. During these years he wrote *The Tooth of Crime*, a play that demonstrated his originality and command of language more completely than anything else he had written. With an apparently firmer sense of himself and his art, he returned to the United States and began a phase of his career that has brought him national prominence.

IV. The Family: "Fist Fights across the Table"

Much of Sam Shepard's fame and reputation rests on the work he has done since 1977. In that year *Curse of the Starving Class* was awarded an Obie for best new play, the first time Shepard had won in that category, and two years later, *Buried Child* received the Pulitzer Prize as well as an Obie for distinguished play. In 1978 Shepard began acting in films when he played the wealthy farmer in Terence Malik's *Days of Heaven*. *True West*, which Shepard has identified along with *Curse of the Starving Class* and *Buried Child* as constituting a "family trilogy," opened at the Magic Theatre in San Francisco in 1980 and was subsequently staged with great success in Chicago and New York and, finally, for public television. Acting roles in the films *Raggedy Man*, *Resurrection*, *Frances*, and *The Right Stuff* have made his name known among a larger general public, while his latest play, *Fool for Love*, has reinforced his preeminent position in the American theater.

The immediate lineage of *Curse of the Starving Class* can be traced back to Shepard's first extant play, *The Rock Garden*, and through all his plays that deal with father/son relationships, especially *The Holy Ghostly*. More than any of the earlier plays, however, *Curse* generalizes its subjects by using the condition of the family as a metaphor for the human condition itself, which dooms everyone to be a carrier and transmitter of the poisons of past generations. In this light and on the larger scale of Western drama, *Curse of the Starving Class*, as part of the family trilogy, has been called one of "Shepard's attempts at Greek tragedy."[1]

In the theatrical world of Sam Shepard, family life is like all life, violent and contradictory, shaped by long-suppressed forces and dark secrets. Although the fields of the

1. Ruby Cohn, *New American Dramatics: 1960–1980* (New York: Grove Press, 1982), p. 183.

family farm may be "green lush wet dripping corn bacon and tomatoes the size of your fist," inside the house there are fist "fights across the table brother fights father and wife fights father son fights sister brother fights the priest."[2] The environment is binding and imprisoning, with the characters wrenched between the demands of socialized conduct and the curse of more primitive, natural behavior. In such an environment the members of the family devour each other in relationships based on exploitation, alienation, and lies.

Curse of the Starving Class begins in the aftermath of an act of violence. Wesley, the son, is cleaning up the pieces of a screen door that his father, Weston, destroyed in a drunken rage the night before. The psychological significance of the event is revealed in a monologue that Wesley delivers during a conversation he has been having with his mother, Ella, who had locked the door to prevent Weston from getting in. Speaking as if he were a child and breaking the naturalistic interaction that has been taking place in his talk with Ella, Wesley describes himself lying in bed:

> I could feel the space around me like a big, black world. I listened like an animal. My listening was afraid. . . . My heart was pounding. Just from my Dad coming back. . . . Foot kicking hard through the door. One foot right through door. Bottle crashing. Glass breaking. Fist through door. Man cursing. Man going insane. . . . Woman screaming. Mom screaming. Mom screaming for police. Man throwing wood. Man throwing up. Mom calling cops. Dad crashing away. . . . Heart still pounding. No sound. Mom crying soft. Soft crying. Then no sound.

Buried in the grown son are the childhood fears and antagonisms that help determine his present relationship to his father and, along with them, the seeds of his father's nature that at any moment may begin to germinate. Later in the play, Weston describes this connection between father and son as a poison that one generation picks up from another. Wesley sees the poison in Weston just as Weston

2. *Hawk Moon*, p. 68.

saw it in his father, though only after it was too late, only after he himself had become infected with it. By the end of the play, it is clear that Wesley also carries the poison in him and by implication is doomed to pass it on.

In addition to giving psychological information, Wesley's monologue effectively isolates him from the rest of the family. While he is speaking, Ella goes about her own business, looking for a pan and cooking bacon, paying no attention to what Wesley is saying. At the conclusion of his monologue, Ella begins one of her own, speaking as if to her daughter, Emma, though Emma is not present. Suggesting one of the meanings of *curse* in the play, she counsels Emma not to be afraid of her first period. "I want you to know all the facts before you go off and pick up a lot of lies," she tells her. Characteristic of relations in the family, however, Ella immediately lies herself: "Now, the first thing is that you should never go swimming when that happens. It can cause you to bleed to death. The water draws it out of you." At the conclusion of this remark, Emma enters and picks up on Ella's comment as if she has been part of the conversation from the beginning. Lies; thoughts, feelings, and words existing in a vacuum; lack of any real contact or understanding: these are the substance of Shepard's American family.

This underlying deceptiveness and emotional barrenness make the family part of the starving class and constitute another kind of curse. At first, however, the members of the family cannot see themselves in these terms. Defining class economically, rather than psychologically (or perhaps even philosophically) as Shepard means it, Emma insists on maintaining some kind of respectable social status. Looking into the empty refrigerator, where earlier she had stored a chicken to use for a 4–H demonstration but which Ella had cooked, Emma says comically, though with serious intent, "Hello? Anything in there? We're not broke you know, so you don't have to hide! . . . We're not part of the starving class!" Wesley makes a similar statement a short time later when he brings a sick lamb into the house and builds a pen for it in the middle of the kitchen. "You're lucky I'm not really starving," he says to the lamb. "You're lucky this is a civilized household." Later, when Wesley comes firmly under control of the curse, he butchers the lamb, justifying his action to Weston by saying, "We need some food." Ironically, Weston, who is most responsible for Wesley's newfound insight into their true condition, but who himself wants to start his life over again and rebuild the family, rejects Wesley's action. "You couldn't be all that starving!" he tells him. "We're not that bad off, goddamnit! I've seen starving people in my time, and we're not that bad off!"

The empty refrigerator, that sign of the family's deep-rooted starvation, becomes the focal point of the action again when Weston finally makes his entrance at the end of act 1. He is carrying a bag full of artichokes, which he tells Wesley he has picked "up for half-price out in Hot Springs." Seeing himself as "MR. SLAVE LABOR . . . COME HOME TO REPLENISH THE EMPTY LARDER," he only succeeds in replenishing the family's supply of primitive wildness that contradicts its veneer of socialized behavior. When Ella returns home in act 2 with a bag of groceries, she throws Weston's artichokes out of the refrigerator and onto the floor. Out of this conflict of artichokes and groceries, and sparked by Wesley's comment to Ella that Weston has threatened to kill her, Ella tries to define the nature of the curse that hangs over them:

> I can feel it. It's invisible but it's there. It's always there. It comes onto us like nighttime. . . . And it always comes. Re-peats itself. It comes even when you do everything to stop it from coming. . . . And it goes back. Deep. . . . To tiny little swimming things making up their minds without us. Plot-ting in the womb. Before that even. In the air. We're sur-rounded with it. . . . It goes forward too. We spread it. We pass it on. . . . It goes on and on like that without us.

Although the description appears at first to be a genetic one, the curse cannot be described that concretely. The curse is beyond genetics, beyond original sin, and, finally, perhaps beyond explanation. Whatever its source, it de-fines the human condition and is doomed to be repeated.

Into the explosive situation of this family enters Taylor,

the representative of some unidentified land developers. In the past he fast-talked Weston into buying a worthless piece of desert property, and now he has convinced Ella to sell everything: "the house, the land, the orchard, the tractor, the stock." Taylor brings with him another kind of curse, the curse that is destroying the old West and replacing it with house-to-house shopping centers. Wesley explains to Emma the real significance of Taylor's interest in their house:

> He works for an agency. Land development. . . . So it means more than losing a house. It means losing a country. . . . It's a zombie invasion. Taylor is the head zombie. . . . He's only a sign that more zombies are on their way. . . . There'll be bulldozers crashing through the orchard. . . . There'll be steel girders spanning acres of land. Cement pilings. Prefab walls. Zombie architecture, owned by invisible zombies, built by zombies for the use and convenience of all other zombies. A zombie city! Right here! Right where we're living now.

For Taylor this devouring of the land is "investment in the future," but for Wesley it is the end of the past. He tells Emma that he has been thinking of going to Alaska, and when she asks him, "What's in Alaska?," he replies, "The frontier." Emma thinks Wesley's plan is crazy, but he justifies it by telling her, "It's full of possibilities." This notion of the frontier, though it is more mythic and poetic than historical, functions in Shepard's plays as a powerful image of the unconstrained life and may stem from Frederick Jackson Turner's famous thesis on the significance of the frontier, a place which Turner saw as "the meeting point between savagery and civilization."[3]

For Shepard the idea of the frontier provides a metaphor for that contradiction of the civilized and the savage that exists on the personal level within the individual and on the social level within the family and the nation. When Emma first meets Taylor, she warns him of what her father might do if he comes home and finds Taylor there: "He's

3. *The Frontier in American History* (New York: Henry Holt and Company, 1953), p. 3.

got a terrible temper. He almost killed one guy he caught her with. . . . A short fuse they call it. Runs in the family. His father was just like him. And his father before him. Wesley is just like Pop, too. Like liquid dynamite. . . . It's the same thing that makes him drink. . . . Highly explosive." Weston describes himself and his reaction to Taylor in the same terms: "He doesn't know what he's dealing with. He thinks I'm just like him. . . . He's not counting on what's in my blood. He doesn't realize the explosiveness. We don't belong to the same class. . . . He's counting on me to use my reason. . . . He's not counting on murder."

The possibility for explosion born out of this natural, as opposed to socialized, part of the self hangs over the entire play, as it does over most of Shepard's plays, including *Buried Child* and *True West*, which complete the family trilogy. It is seen in Weston's breaking down of the screen door, in Wesley's slaughtering of the lamb, in Emma's shooting up of the Alibi Club (an act that Emma earlier in the play would have considered herself incapable of and that Weston takes pride in because it shows that she has courage to get charged up about something), in Slater's and Emerson's blowing up of the car, and in the telling of two stories about an eagle, one told by Weston and the other by Ella.

Weston's story of the eagle opens act 3 and is significant not only because of the sudden appearance of the wild and natural, but also because of Weston's own longing to be free of the everydayness and regularity of family life. He describes an incident that occurred while he was castrating lambs. An eagle began to swoop down in an attempt to grab the testes, and Weston obliged him by throwing some of them onto the roof of the shed. Each time the eagle came down, Weston cheered for him, getting an "icy feeling" in his backbone, a feeling he had not experienced since the first time he "went up in a B–49." Ironically, this story begins the act in which Weston cleans himself up and talks about renewing his family life, though by the end Weston leaves again, presumably on his way to Mexico to escape the wrath of his creditors and to "start a whole new life down there."

Ella's story ends act 3, and although she identifies it as one that Weston used to tell, it is a different story. From her perspective, however, this second version is equally significant. Hers is a story of mutual destruction in which the eagle comes down not after lamb testes but after a cat. With the cat clutched in the eagle's talons, a battle of the wild and the domesticated takes place high in the air: "They fight like crazy in the middle of the sky. The cat's tearing his chest out, and the eagle's trying to drop him, but the cat won't let go because he knows if he falls he'll die. . . . And they come crashing down to the earth. Both of them come crashing down. Like one whole thing." With this story the play ends, leaving the family in much the same condition as the eagle and the cat.

Four months after the New York premiere of *Curse of the Starving Class*, the Magic Theatre in San Francisco presented *Buried Child*. The picture of the American family that this second play in the trilogy presents is even darker than the one that preceded it. Set on an unproductive farm in Illinois among people whose alienated lives are controlled by a terrible secret from the past, *Buried Child* is the antithesis of the Norman Rockwell image of rural life. Its contradictory and ambiguous web of relationships and events defies easy explanation and turns its essentially realistic setting into a moral and psychological battleground.

Like *Curse of the Starving Class*, the roots of *Buried Child* can be found as far back as *The Rock Garden*. Its very first image is one of separation and incommunicability. Dodge, a man in his seventies, sits on a sofa staring at a television, which emits only a flickering light. He is covered by a blanket, and occasionally he reaches under a pillow for a bottle of whiskey, from which he takes furtive swigs. His wife, Halie, talks to him from upstairs (offstage) about the rain. They often have to yell because of the distance between them (a sign of their much deeper separation), but for the most part Dodge simply allows Halie to talk while he either ignores what she says or mimics it sarcastically.

The isolation of characters that is represented in the separation of Dodge and Halie into onstage and offstage spaces is intensified by the appearance of Tilden, the couple's oldest son. In the stage directions, Shepard indicates that "something about him is profoundly burned out and displaced." In addition, Tilden introduces an element that makes any straightforward reading of the action impossible; he carries an armload of corn, which he says he picked "right out back," even though Dodge says nothing has been planted there since 1935. Like Weston's artichokes, the corn must be seen as a sign, in this case of Tilden's relationship to the past. Dodge later denies even the existence of the past, but Tilden lives in it and even brings in vegetables from the fields of the past. As if to emphasize the abstract function of the corn, Shepard has Halie react to its presence in the middle of the living room with a question that will be answered only later in the play: "What's the meaning of this corn Tilden!" His response does not provide an explanation, but it does create an image, his standing in the middle of the corn, that recurs significantly in act 3 in the form of a photograph from childhood that becomes part of the mechanism by which Halie's question is answered.

Tilden's mental condition is paralleled by the physical disability of his younger brother Bradley, who had his leg amputated by a chain saw at some indefinite time in the past. When Halie tells Dodge that Bradley is coming over to give him a haircut, Dodge becomes quite upset: "Last time he left me almost bald!" Although it is never spelled out, Bradley's action is clearly aggression against his father, a sort of amputation. Becoming more adamant, Dodge insists that he will not let Bradley in: "Bradley doesn't even live here!. . . . He was born in a goddamn hog wallow!. . . He doesn't belong in this house." Halie is shocked by this remark and asks Dodge how he can say that about his "own flesh and blood." Dodge's response brings the first mention of the secret that haunts the family, the secret of the buried child: "He's not my flesh and blood! My flesh and blood's buried in the back yard!" The meaning of this assertion is by no means clear, especially since it is contradicted by things said later in the play; it is simply one of a number of assertions that must be taken together and understood on a level other than that of objective fact. In the final analysis, the buried child of the title signifies a set of familial attitudes and relationships more than it does an individual or a particular event from the past.

Similar to the mysterious buried child is the shadowy figure of another dead child, Ansel, who apparently died on his honeymoon, though Halie persists in thinking he was murdered by his Italian wife and her family. To Halie, Ansel was the best of the three sons: "He was a hero. . . . A genuine hero. . . . Ansel could've been a great man. One of the greatest. . . . It's not fitting for a man like that to die in a motel room." Halie speaks of having a monument built to him, "a big, tall statue with a basketball in one hand and a rifle in the other." By Halie's own testimony, however, Ansel died before he could have become a soldier, and according to Bradley, Ansel never played basketball, even though Halie insists that he did. The contradictions call into question the very existence of Ansel, suggesting that he is no more than Halie's projection of the ideal son.

Act 2 begins with the arrival of Vince, Tilden's son. With his girlfriend, Shelly, he is on his way to New Mexico to see his father, not realizing that he will find him in Illinois. Wearing jeans, boots, and a plaid shirt, and carrying a saxophone case, Vince combines the image of the cowboy and the musician and suggests Shepard himself. He is on a journey to reestablish his roots, to find his past and his place in the life of the family. As Shelly describes their trip, "We had to stop off at every tiny little meatball town that he remembered from his boyhood! Every stupid little donut shop he ever kissed a girl in. Every Drive-In. Every Drag Strip. Every football field he ever broke a bone on."

Contrary to what Vince expects, Dodge does not recognize him, going so far as to deny that he is anybody's grandfather. This denial does not represent the old man's forgetfulness but rather his conscious rejection of family ties. For example, he admonishes Tilden: "You shouldn't be needing your parents at your age. It's unnatural. . . . I never went back to my parents. Never. Never even had the urge." Later, he tells Shelly, "You think just because people propagate they have to love their offspring? You never seen a bitch eat her puppies?" Although Vince is shocked by this rejection, he later does the same thing himself. Returning home drunk, he refuses recognition from both Dodge and Halie, asking them, "Who are you people?" The cycle of rejection comes full circle, and Vince takes on the characteristics of alienation that were initially seen in Dodge.

Shortly after Vince's arrival and his first encounter with Dodge, Tilden enters, but Vince cannot gain recognition from his father either. Instead, Tilden responds, "I had a son once but we buried him." This remark has a double meaning: it refers metaphorically to Vince's position in the family and literally to another child, born to Halie but killed by Dodge and buried in the field behind the house. The exact story regarding this child is never made clear. Dodge first says that his flesh and blood is buried in the backyard, but he claims that the child he killed and buried was not his:

> Halie had this kid. This baby boy. . . . I let her have it on her own. All the other boys I had had the best doctors, best nurses, everything. This one I let her have by herself. This one hurt real bad. Almost killed her, but she had it anyway. It lived, see. . . . It wanted to grow up in this family. It wanted to be just like us. It wanted to pretend that I was its father. She wanted me to believe in it. Even when everyone around us knew. Everyone. All our boys knew. Tilden knew.

This reference to Tilden suggests that he may have been the father of his mother's child, especially since he has already said that he had a son whom he had buried. Dodge stresses the implication about Tilden when he remarks that Tilden knew about the child "better than any of us" and when he describes how Tilden used to "walk for miles with that kid in his arms." Dodge also emphasizes the illicit nature of the child in his explanation of why he killed it: "We couldn't let a thing like that continue. We couldn't allow that to grow up right in the middle of our lives. It made everything we'd accomplished look like it was nothin'. Everything was cancelled out by this one mistake. This one weakness." This implication, however—and in fact the entire story—is contradicted by an earlier claim made by Dodge that the child was buried before Tilden was even born. Finally, Halie declares Dodge's whole story to be a lie.

The mystery of the child is further deepened by a photograph that Shelly finds of Halie and the children standing in the corn. She describes how Halie has a baby in her arms but is looking at it as if "it didn't even belong to her." To this remark Dodge responds angrily, "That's about enough outa' you!" His attempt to silence Shelly indicates that she has touched a sensitive nerve. Is this the child that Dodge killed, and what does the look on Halie's face signify? If this is one of the other children, is it Tilden, Ansel, or Bradley? To Shelly, Dodge's attitude is incomprehensible, and she asks, "What's happened to this family anyway?" The only answer that Dodge supplies is that he has spawned a lot of children and that there is nothing to remember about any of them. If she is interested in the family, she should ask Halie, who has "traced it all the way back to the grave." In this context, Dodge's unusual remark is precise in its meaning because the true history of this family begins at the grave of the buried child.

Near the end of act 2, Vince leaves to buy a bottle of whiskey for Dodge, forcing Shelly to remain behind and deal with the situation as best she can. When he finally returns the next morning (halfway through act 3), he is drunk and, like Weston in *Curse of the Starving Class*, enters violently, smashing bottles on the porch of the house. Ironically, this kind of entrance brings recognition. Halie instantly knows who he is, and Dodge, in a verbal will, names his "Grandson, Vincent" as his heir. The appropriateness of this action becomes clear as Vince begins to account for his whereabouts the night before. He describes himself in almost identical terms to those used by Dodge to explain his lack of interest in the family history:

> I drove all night. . . . I could see myself in the windshield. . . . I studied my face. Studied everything about it. As though I was looking at another man. As though I could see his whole race behind him. . . . I saw him dead and alive at the same time. . . . And then his face changed. His face

became his father's face. Same bones. Same eyes. Same nose. Same breath. And his father's face changed to his Grandfather's face. And it went on like that. . . . Clear back to faces I'd never seen before but still recognized. . . . Straight back as far as they'd take me. Then it all dissolved.

For Dodge, it does not matter how far back the line can be traced because there is nothing but "a long line of corpses."

At the heart of this speech is that curse passed on from father to son that makes them both similar to and profoundly alienated from each other. Dodge refuses to be father to his sons, and as a result one is a burned-out shell, another is mutilated, and a third is dead. A mysterious fourth is buried in the field behind the house, while Vince, the grandson, is doomed to continue a line of corpses, the image of a creator who has denied him. Vince's search for a father ends at the grave of a child who, in truth, had no father.

As the play draws to a close, Vince crosses to Dodge and discovers that he is dead, a death that had come "completely unnoticed." In the house that is now his, Vince lies on the sofa, positioning himself to become like Dodge. Halie begins to talk from upstairs, announcing that she can see the corn growing, that Tilden was right after all. As she continues to talk, Tilden enters carrying the body of the dead child, which he has just dug out of the earth. In contrast to the gruesome aspects of this scene, however, Halie's monologue suggests renewal and growth: "You can't force a thing to grow. You can't interfere with it. It's all hidden. It's all unseen. You just gotta wait til it pops up out of the ground. Tiny little shoot. . . . Strong though. Strong enough to break the earth even. It's a miracle."

In this light, the metaphor of the buried child begins to shift its meaning. From a representation of all that is dark and devouring in the family, it takes on the significance of hope. Dodge may have killed the child, but Tilden nurtured it, and it is for Tilden that the corn and other vegetables grow. The second time that Tilden came in from the fields, he was carrying an armload of carrots, which he gave to Shelly. Vince tried to knock the carrots out of her arms, but she protected them as if protecting a child. Since

143

the carrots came out of the earth in which the child is buried, they can be seen as a metaphor for the child, and the way in which Shelly holds them reinforces this comparison. Correspondingly, Vince's attempt to get the carrots away from Shelly duplicates Dodge's taking of the child from Tilden in order to kill it. Understanding the corn from this perspective answers Halie's question as to its meaning and explains how the fields can be both barren (for Dodge) and fruitful (for Tilden) at the same time. In the last line of the play, Shepard makes a pun that explains the appearance of the mysterious crops. "I've never seen a crop like this is my whole life," says Halie. "Maybe it's the sun. Maybe that's it. Maybe it's the sun." Indeed, it is the son (sun) that motivates these events, that "tiny little shoot" that has been growing unseen but is "strong enough to break the earth."

True West, the third play in the family trilogy, appeared two years after *Buried Child*. It is a "civil war" of family life, a showdown between brothers. In its setting, it is the most realistic of all Shepard's plays, though its hyperbolic events and character development push the play toward abstraction. Like *Curse of the Starving Class* it explores the contradictions, in both the individual and the family, between socialized and unsocialized behavior, rationality and unbridled emotion, words and action, confinement and freedom. In the background is the image of the absent father, living in the desert and completely withdrawn from normal social contact, while in the foreground, always present, is a potential for violence that threatens to rip the delicate fabric of social interaction that prevents two brothers with radically different lives from killing each other.

The entire action of the play takes place in "a kitchen and adjoining alcove of an older home in a Southern California suburb, about 40 miles east of Los Angeles." The home belongs to the mother of the two main characters, Austin, an Ivy League–educated screenwriter, and Lee, a drifter who has recently been living on the desert. Mom is letting Austin use the house while she is in Alaska on vacation. To Austin's dismay, Lee has shown up unexpectedly and intends to stay for awhile. Lee has a tattered, violent look that contrasts sharply with Austin's preppiness and reserve. From the very beginning they clash.

Austin has come to his mother's house in order to work on a film outline for a producer named Saul Kimmer. Lee spends most of his time just hanging around, though he also cases the neighborhood for houses to rob. Their conversations range freely over the past, their father, the current status of their lives, and the way in which this part of the country has been built up since they were kids.

Returning to the house with a stolen television, Lee interrupts a conference between Austin and Saul and soon has Saul agreeing to play a game of golf with him. The game leads to Saul's getting sold on Lee's idea for a modern Western, an idea that Saul wants Austin to turn into a screenplay. Although Austin balks at doing it, he finds that he has no choice if he wants to continue his own project.

Saul is attracted to Lee's project because it has "something about the real West . . . something about the land." To this, Austin responds, "He's been camped out on the desert for three months. . . . What's he knew about what people wanna' see on the screen! I drive on the freeway every day. I swallow the smog. I watch the news in color. I shop in the Safeway. I'm the one who's in touch! Not him!" Getting nowhere with this line of argument, Austin takes a different tack: "There's no such thing as the West anymore! It's a dead issue!"

In one way Austin is right; the West of myth and legend is dead. Whether it ever existed is questionable, but it is evident that the West of today does not measure up to it, that is, up to the myth. If the true West still exists, it probably has to do with the land, as Saul so inarticulately suggests. When Austin talks to Lee about how the area in which they were raised has been built up, Lee responds that it has been more than built up, it has been "wiped out." Austin has learned to live in this wiped-out landscape, with its freeways, Safeways, and smog, but Lee has not. Instead, he has been spending his time in the Mojave Desert, and to that extent his wanderings have been a search for the true West. He clearly links himself to this search when he recommends that Saul see the film *Lonely Are the Brave*, in which Kirk Douglas plays a westerner out of his time, a man who tries to maintain an independent life in the open country, but who, ironically, gets run down by a trailer truck while crossing a highway on his horse.

The script idea that Lee has presented to Saul complements both the Kirk Douglas film and the relationship between Austin and Lee. It is about one man chasing another across the prairie, first in trucks and then on horseback. The conflict between the two men parallels the conflict between the two brothers, while the change from truck to horse signifies the longing for the old West. The basic nature of the story and of the coincidental material that Lee insists on adding as the writing progresses so offends Austin's sense of screenwriting that he repeatedly interrupts Lee's outlining of the plot. 'It's not like real life!" he insists. "Things don't happen like that." Since Lee is really describing his own desire to be free, however, the events of the story seem perfectly acceptable to him. Unlike Austin, Lee's problem is not with what to say, but with how to say it. This, of course, is one of the fundamental problems of the writer, and Shepard gives it a particularly comic aspect when Lee objects to one of his own lines because it sounds like a cliché when Austin reads it back to him. "I know this prairie like the back a' my hand," reads Austin. To Lee's response that the line is stupid, Austin suggests the alternative, "I'm on intimate terms with this prairie." Although he does not know how to react at first, Lee finally decides that the line is original. "That has a real ring to it," he concludes.

The true West and the way to describe it is indeed elusive, as is the correct relationship between brothers. For Austin the fact that they are brothers makes certain acts impossible, but Lee sees the possibilities from a less socially responsible perspective. "You go down to the L.A. Police Department there and ask them what kinda' people kill each other the most," he tells Austin. "Family people. Brothers. Brothers-in-law. Cousins. Real American-type people. They kill each other in the heat mostly. . . . Right

146

about this time a' year." By the end of the play, Austin and Lee are on the verge of killing each other, but for the time being, violence remains just below the surface, and the reasons behind their conflict either remain repressed or get transposed into Lee's film story.

Particularly revealing of the relationship between the brothers is a descriptive paragraph from Lee's film outline that ends act 1:

> So they take off after each other straight into an endless black prairie. The sun is just comin' down and they can feel the night on their backs. What they don't know is that each one of 'em is afraid, see. Each one separately thinks that he's the only one that's afraid. And they keep ridin' like that. . . . And the one who's chasin' doesn't know where the other one is taking him. And the one who's being chased doesn't know where he's going.

As the brothers struggle with each other verbally, and finally physically, they enter a territory where anything is possible. Their conflict is as old as that of Cain and Abel, and the feeling of death on their backs is as strong as the fears that drive them. Which is the pursuer and which the pursued? In relation to Austin and Lee, the question loses its meaning, for it belongs more to the simplified realms of myth and the movies. In the West of contemporary reality, which may be the only true West, it is not so easy to tell the pursuer from the pursued, to decide between the bad guys and the good guys, to separate the acceptable from the unacceptable or the socialized from the primitive. As the deserts into which one can flee give way to suburban development, the old frontier, Turner's "hither edge of free land," is more and more transformed into a myth of freedom that can no longer be realized, with the result that "the meeting point between savagery and civilization" is internalized and defines the contours of a purely inner true West.

A turning point occurs in the play when Austin accepts a challenge from Lee to steal something without getting caught. The next morning, Austin has a line of toasters on the kitchen counter, the loot of his night's work in going from house to house in the neighborhood. Although Lee thinks that stealing so many toasters is "the dumbest thing" he has ever seen, the act represents for Austin a threshold of experience that opens up a new world of possibilities. When Lee asks him for the time, Austin gives an answer that functions as a metaphor for the potential dangers that he faces now that he has taken a step away from his safe round of respectable daily routines: "This is the time of morning when the coyotes kill people's cocker spaniels. Did you hear them? That's what they were doing out there. Luring innocent pets away from their homes." Like the cocker spaniels, Austin is being lured into the more open-ended and violent world of his brother.

Taking the next step, Austin asks Lee, "What if I come with you out to the desert?" To Lee, who lives in the desert out of something more akin to necessity than to choice, Austin's query is crazy: "Here, you are down here, rollin' in bucks. Floatin' up and down in elevators. And you wanna' learn how to live on the desert!" Rational as Lee's line of argument is, it no longer applies to Austin in the way it once might have. His contact with Lee and his confrontation with a powerful strain of alienation and violence in his family has weakened his ties to normal social behavior and called into question the ambitions that have been motivating him. "There's nothin' down here for me," he insists. "There never was. . . . There's nothin' real down here, Lee! Least of all me!"

Like one of the cowboys in the movie chase scene, Lee responds from the fearful position of a man who does not know where he is going: "Hey, do you actually think I chose to live out in the middle a' nowhere? Do ya'? Ya' think it's some kinda' philosophical decision I took or somethin'? I'm livin' out there 'cause I can't make it here!" Nevertheless, he agrees to take Austin with him if Austin will finish the movie outline for him. This plan is interrupted, however, by Mom's unexpected return from Alaska.

By this time in the play, the house is in shambles. As a result of the brothers' constant conflicts, the kitchen and alcove are littered with toasters, pieces of bread that Austin had put in them, the contents of the kitchen drawers spilled out by Lee while looking for a pencil, Austin's smashed typewriter (which Lee attacked with a golf club), and numerous beer cans. In addition, all of Mom's plants, which Austin was supposed to water, have died. To this display of her sons' psychic and social confusion, Mom casually and absently asks, "What happened in here?" After looking around more, she finally musters a laconic "Well it's one hell of a mess in here isn't it?" This spacey response, apparently characteristic of her relationship with her sons, is topped by her insistence that they must all rush to the museum to see Picasso, who the newspapers say is going to be in town. Not even Austin's telling her that Picasso is dead can turn her from this idea. Finally, Austin changes the direction of the conversation by announcing that he is going away with Lee.

Mom reacts to this with a surprise that puts the plan in a new perspective for Lee. He suddenly backs out of the agreement, causing Austin to enter fully into his new world of unsocialized behavior. Wrapping the telephone cord around his hands, he attacks Lee from behind and tightens the cord around his neck. In her usual uninvolved manner, Mom tells Austin, "Well you can't kill him." But he can, of course. He has reached that position Lee described earlier in which murder within the family becomes common. "I can kill him!" he says. "I can easily kill him. Right now. Right here." Mom's response is to pick up her bags and leave, announcing that being in her home under these conditions "is worse than being homeless." With Mom gone, Austin tries to make a deal with Lee, being given a head start in exchange for letting go of the cord, but Lee does not respond. He lies motionless on the floor—until without warning he springs to his feet. Blocking the exit, Lee squares off for the final confrontation. A coyote is heard (luring another cocker spaniel to his death?) as the lights fade and "the figures of the brothers . . . appear to be caught in a vast desert-like landscape." Austin has gotten his wish, and there is no turning back.

The family trilogy finally propelled Shepard into the limelight. It brought him a Pulitzer Prize and three Obie

Awards, including one for the "sustained achievement" of his writing career. Although the Pulitzer Prize was the most prestigious award, the Obie for "sustained achievement" was really the most significant because it recognized more than just the three most recent plays, instead citing Shepard's entire body of work, which for sixteen years had been helping to regenerate the American theater. This recognition was especially appropriate since among the pre-trilogy plays are several, including *The Mad Dog Blues*, *The Tooth of Crime*, and *Angel City*, that must be considered essential works of contemporary drama. On a more popular level of recognition, Shepard also launched his screen acting career with major roles in *Days of Heaven* (1978) and *Resurrection* (1980), an activity that—ironically, given his attitude toward the film industry—has also brought him to the threshold of stardom.

Following the premiere of *Buried Child*, Shepard and actor/director Joseph Chaikin collaborated in San Francisco for three weeks on a theater piece for voice and percussion instruments called *Tongues*. They then staged the piece at the Magic Theatre, with Chaikin performing the words and Shepard the music. Although Shepard has acknowledged that others performing *Tongues* would have to develop their own staging and working method, he did comment on the intentions behind the piece: "The various voices are not so much intended to be caricatures as they are attitudes or impulses, constantly shifting and sliding into each other, sometimes abruptly, sometimes slowly, seemingly out of nowhere. Likewise, the music is not intended to make comments on the voice but to support these changing impulses, to make temporary environments for the voice to live in."[4]

Tongues is the essence of theater, at least from Shepard's perspective, because it is language unimpeded by spectacle and therefore free, free to create drama without dramatic form, characterization without characters, and story without action. It does so through a series of fifteen speak-

4. "Introduction to *Tongues*," in Sam Shepard, *Seven Plays* (New York: Bantam Books, 1981), p. 302.

ers or voices that cover a wide range of human experience. Appropriate to the period in which it was written and performed, the period of the family trilogy, the first speaker defines the condition of being born into, living with, and dying out of a social group. It begins as each individual human life must begin: "He was born in the middle of a story which he had nothing to do with. / In the middle of a people." And everything that happens to him happens in terms of the people. "He was honored. / He was dishonored. / He was married. / He became old. / He became older." Until finally he hears "a voice he's never heard." And this voice separates him from the people. "You are entirely dead. / What is unfinished is forever unfinished. / What happened has happened. / You are entirely gone from the people."

From its beginning, which gives an overview of a life, the piece goes on to individual voices at different stages or in different conditions: a worker's voice talking about a new job and hope for advancement; a mother's voice describing the first touching and holding of a newborn child; a calling voice trying to capture some essence of itself upon which its identity seems to rest; a voice speaking to a blind person that tries to describe the blind person's position in a space and to link what is going on inside him to what is going on outside; the voices of two hungry ones, each too polite to mention it on the assumption that the other is not hungry; an invocation of a spirit outside time, space, and action; a voice from the dead that comes in response to the invocation; an inquiry to the dead one seeking information about death; a singing voice in exaggerated 1940s style; a series of letter-writing voices; a pompous voice left speechless by some incident; a public voice as if a politician speaking to constituents; a voice speaking to one about to die but not knowing what to say; and, finally, a simple, direct voice that remembers and reconstructs things that happened during the day and that, ironically, in remembering a tree blossoming, speaks of the need to learn the tree's language, a language "without a word."

Having worked together successfully on *Tongues*, Shepard and Chaikin collaborated on a new piece the following year. "Before meeting," wrote Chaikin, "we decided that our piece should be about romantic love and about the closeness and distance between lovers." The result, *Savage/Love*, had a working method somewhat different from that used for *Tongues*. Continuing Chaikin's account, "The first step was to choose the moments, and then to speak from within those moments. A 'moment' could be the first instant of meeting the lover, or it could be the experience of lovers sleeping next to one another, with one a little bit awake watching the other one sleep. Unlike our approach to 'Tongues,' I would improvise around or inside a moment; Sam would write. We would later discuss and try things."[5]

The piece contains nineteen of these moments, each with a title that defines its essential nature: of first encounter, with its attendant hope and wondering; of listening and not listening; of the inability to find the words to express feelings; of the clichéd use of endearing terms; of presenting oneself to another; of begging, getting no response, becoming guarded, and finally turning hostile; of being haunted by the sense of someone not there; and of a number of other feelings and actions including accusation, pretense, absence, fulfillment, and the bridging of separation.

Although Shepard's and Chaikin's working methods may have differed for each of the pieces they collaborated on, *Savage/Love* shares with *Tongues* a commitment to language. In that sense both pieces can be seen as paradigms for Shepard's aspirations as a dramatist. Stripped of the usual trappings of a play, these theater pieces reveal the essential nature of drama in a theatrical setting, especially in relation to characterization. By eliminating characters and their actions, Shepard puts in relief the source from which these elements flow, the language which has "the capacity to evoke visions in the eye of the audience."[6]

Shepard's most recent play, *Fool for Love*, is a flawless blending of stylization and verisimilitude, the work of a

---

5. "Introduction to *Savage/Love*," in *Seven Plays*, p. 322.
6. "Language, Visualization, and the Inner Library," p. 216.

dramatist in full command of his medium and at the height of his artistic powers. In addition, the original production at the Magic Theatre was staged by the author and shows clearly that Shepard is not only the premier playwright of the American theater but also one of its most accomplished directors.

In his introduction to the play, Shepard indicates that it "is to be performed relentlessly without a break." And indeed it is a relentless work, a play that moves insistently from one end of its dramatic conflict to the other, that works not only off the power of its language but also from an extraordinary rendering of all psychological elements as externalized physical action. Throughout the play the two main characters throw their bodies into the walls of the set, slam doors, crash to the floor and crawl and slide across it, move violently toward each other, and occasionally resort to physical abuse. Shepard even indicates that the set should be rigged to emphasize the extreme physicality of the movements: "The door is amplified with microphones and a bass drum hidden in the frame so that each time an actor slams it, the door booms loud and long." In addition, the stage directions specify precise gestural and movement instructions for the actors that force them to externalize inner states. For example: "She erupts furiously, leaping off bed and lashing out at him with her fists"; "She grabs pillow, clutching it to her chest then throws herself face down on bed, moaning and moving from one end of bed to the other on her elbows and knees"; "He bangs his head into wall"; "He laughs, crosses to table, takes a deep drink from bottle, cocks his head back, gargles, swallows, then does a back flip across stage and crashes into stage right wall."

The action of the play is set in a shabby motel on the edge of the Mojave Desert. Although the space is essentially realistic, the nature and placement of the furniture (a cast-iron bed just off center stage and a formica-top metal kitchen with two chairs down left) give the room an abstracted quality. In addition, a large picture window in the center of the upstage wall, revealing only a suffused yellow-orange light from the outside, suggests a world beyond the room, but in such a mediated way that it exists as a conceptual rather than as an actual space.

The audience's first contact is with the set itself; no actors are present. The lights fade to black, and in the darkness the song "Wake Up" by country star Merle Haggard is heard. As the lights come back up, three of the play's four characters are seen. May is sitting on the edge of the bed, staring at the floor; Eddie sits at the table, looking at May; and on a platform extending off the stage down left, sitting in a rocking chair, is the old man. Although he is a constant observer of the action and at times even interacts with Eddie and May, Shepard indicates that "he exists only in the minds" of the other two. For his part, the old man "treats them as though they all existed in the same time and place."

Eddie, a stunt man and rodeo cowboy with the usual wanderlust and dreams of the male protagonist of a Shepard play, has just driven, by his account, 2,480 miles to see May, who now lives in this run-down motel and works as a short-order cook. They have been lovers since high school, though Eddie repeatedly leaves May for varying periods of time, a pattern which has been going on for fifteen years. They are also half brother and sister, having different mothers but, in the old man, the same father. Eddie once again wants May to go away with him, this time to a ranch he says he has in Wyoming. May is fed up with Eddie and no longer believes him when he says he loves her. She is also jealous of a European countess whom she thinks Eddie has been seeing. With contradictory fervor, she tells Eddie that she does not need him anymore, while at the same time she prevents him from leaving. Outside in the parking lot is the countess waiting in a black Mercedes that she periodically drives past the window. At one point she apparently shoots the windshield out of Eddie's truck; later, she sets it on fire.

Eddie is Shepard's latest incarnation of the cowboy figure and of the son who exhibits the characteristics of his father. He is also one of Shepard's representations of the artist. "I thought you were supposed to be a fantasist," says the old man. "Isn't that basically the deal with you?

You dream things up." As the cowboy, Eddie harbors a perpetual desire for an unconstrained life, and as the artist, he creates fictions and therefore may not be telling the truth. In either case, he is unreliable. May is sick of both his wandering and his fantasies, even though she cannot totally free herself from him.

The climax of the play comes when Eddie and May tell two different versions of the same story to Martin, a local handyman and groundskeeper who has come to take May to a movie. May introduces Eddie as her cousin, but while she is out of the room, Eddie reveals that he is actually her brother and her lover. He gives Martin a detailed account of his father's two separate lives and two families, neither of which knew about the other, and of his falling in love with May in high school, having no idea that she was his sister.

At this point, May bolts in from the bathroom where she has been listening to the whole story and declares it to be a lie. She then proceeds to tell her own version, which ends with Eddie's mother committing suicide. At this, the old man leaps up and declares, "That's the dumbest version I ever heard in my whole life." He asks Eddie to represent his side of the story, clearly indicating that the events are being told from two contradictory perspectives, each of which is defined by gender. "I wanna' hear the male side a' this thing," he tells Eddie, but instead, Eddie confirms May's version. As a result of this apparent ability to put aside his male fantasy, May accepts Eddie's assurances that this time things will be different in their relationship.

At the heart of this conflict of stories and this shift of emphasis from the father/son relationship to the man/woman relationship is a new concern in Shepard's writing: to create a female character as dramatically viable as the important male characters of his plays. In describing this change, he has been quoted as saying, "It always seemed to me that there was more mystery to relationships between men, and just now, it's coming to a territory where I'm finding the same mystery between men and women." To express this mystery in a play, however, he had to "sustain a female character and have her remain absolutely true to herself, not only as a social being, but also as an emotional being." In other words, he had to "sustain both sides of the issue" and not make either one of them out to be heroic. "They're just who they are."[7]

If Eddie is to be who he is, then it is necessary that he once again leave May despite what he has promised. Telling her that he is only going outside to check on his horses, he disappears. But May also functions as an independent character, and, realizing immediately that Eddie will not be coming back, she packs her suitcase and sets off on her own. With the flames from Eddie's burning truck lighting the window, the scene slowly fades to black accompanied by Merle Haggard's "I'm the One Who Loves You."

Eddie's behavior toward May parallels the old man's behavior toward Eddie's mother. Both father and son avoid full commitment to a woman: to use the old man's words, neither can "come across for her." When Eddie appears to exchange his fantasy of the past for May's apparently accurate version of it, the old man objects vigorously in terms that clearly separate allegiances: "Stay away from her! . . . You two can't come together! You gotta hold up my end a' this deal! . . . You gotta represent me now! You're my son!" Although momentarily ignoring his father's plea, Eddie cannot escape being his father's son. He might say, along with Weston in *Curse of the Starving Class*, "I just went off for a little while. Now and then. I couldn't stand it here. I couldn't stand the idea that everything would stay the same. . . . I kept looking for it out there somewhere. I kept trying to piece it together."

Eddie is a fantasist, a dreamer of his own life, a cowboy out of time. He is the most finely drawn, and in many ways most typical, of all Shepard's male protagonists. May is the opposite; she is free of fantasies, a realist capable of lasting human commitment, and the only fully developed and significant female character in all of Shepard's work. Together, they represent an interest in character that was largely ab-

7. *New York Times*, 29 January 1984, section 2, p. 26.

sent in the earlier plays. That is not to say that this is a psychological drama in any traditional sense; the staging technique, the abstract qualities of the set, and the style of performance that is indicated by Shepard in the stage directions externalize the play's psychology and create a spectacle that is by no means an analogue of reality. *Fool for Love* is unshamedly theatrical in its coding and fully integrated into Shepard's overall body of work. It is the logical culmination of everything that had come before it, and, with its new interest in creating a female protagonist, perhaps a forecast of what is to come.

V. Destinations

On the cover of *Motel Chronicles* is a photograph of Sam Shepard. He is seen in full length, looking at the camera; his right hand grasps a bottle of Coke, and his left is tucked casually in his pocket. Parked next to him is an old funeral coach with a Texas license plate, and in the background, as if part of another world, the dry, empty street of a small Texas town, washed out by the intense midday sun. Shepard's clothes are well-worn and baggy, perhaps even lived and traveled in for some time. Or are the clothes part of a costume and was the photograph taken during a break in the making of a film? Is Shepard on the road or in character?

Writing about the making of *Resurrection* and the character he was playing, Shepard revealed something about the roles he takes on: "His costume was waiting. It looked just like the clothes he had on, like a deflated version of himself. He switched the clothes he had on for the costume and felt just the same. Exactly the same. Maybe a little bit stiffer. Cleaner maybe too. He wondered if he was supposed to be playing himself. If that's what they hired him for." Later in the same piece, he describes the shooting of a scene on a motorcycle during which he gave up trying to understand the motivations of the character and "just rode the bike and forgot about acting." Finally, taking off on his own, he passed out of camera range and headed down the road at 85 m.p.h., only to skid off the pavement. In forgetting the character, however, Shepard seems to have discovered him: "Suddenly he appeared to himself. He caught himself in a flash. There was no more doubt who the character was." In some way, he was indeed playing himself.[1]

Under the heading *destinations*, Shepard once summarized what appears to be a fundamental condition of his life: "From some place to some place. But in between is

1. *Motel Chronicles*, pp. 10–13.

where the action is."[2] Those moments of action and movement, to which the destinations are only temporary stopping places, include Shepard's plays and film performances as well as his travels. A play or performance is another kind of photograph of the author in which he exchanges his own everyday clothes for those of his artistic creation, but in many ways, the two are "exactly the same." Within limits, all art is a kind of creative biography in which the author and his relation to the world are revealed. Of course, the value of this revelation depends on the quality of the artist's insights and goes beyond the merely biographical, finding its real significance in the human and social conditions to which the artist lends his own personal experience.

Shepard's revealing of himself and his world has struck a responsive chord in audiences both here and abroad. For twenty years his work has painted an inner landscape of his own imaginative response to the personal and social conflicts engendered by the culture that has shaped him. The great significance of Shepard's plays, and the point of contact for their audience, is that this inner landscape is also a profoundly American landscape, rendered memorable, as Ruby Cohn has pointed out, not so much by themes as by images and rhythms.[3] It is his images and rhythms, often drawn from the varied expressions of popular culture and mass media, that also make Shepard uniquely American and intensely modern. Nevertheless, Shepard treats themes that put him in the mainstream of Western literature and twentieth-century drama. For example, Cohn has placed him quite specifically in relation to other American writers: "Like his ancestor O'Neill . . . Shepard in maturity is dramatizing a tragic America, mired in sin. Like the Fitzgerald of *The Great Gatsby*, Shepard is at once seduced by and critical of American wealth and its artefacts. Like Thomas Wolfe, he realizes that you can't go home again—to a pastoral civilization." Making a distinc-

2. *Hawk Moon*, p. 48.
3. *New American Dramatists*, p. 185.

tion, however, she continues: "Like no other American playwright, Shepard enfolds figures of popular culture into more lasting patterns of myth."[4] Out of these myths, he has fashioned a world that is immediate and familiar while still capable of projecting universal meanings.

As a westerner and as a product of popular culture, it was natural for twenty-one-year-old Sam Shepard to utilize the mythic figure of the cowboy for his first play, but it was 1967 before images from popular culture became crucial in Shepard's work. For the next ten years, the plays were dominated by characters and actions taken from movies, rock music, legend, science fiction, current events, and a consumer economy, but with striking originality Shepard endowed the images and traditional mythic figures derived from these sources with new aesthetic vitality while still preserving their established meanings as cultural signs.

Despite Shepard's attempt to put these figures to rest in his 1976 play *Suicide in B♭*, they have continued to exercise an important influence on him. If they have seemed less evident in the work of the past seven or eight years, it is because they have been treated in more realistic contexts and have been reworked in characters that have greater psychological depth and more defined social functions. Eddie in *Fool for Love* is the most recent example, embodying, among other traits, the cowboy figure's wanderlust and rejection of normal social ties.

With *Curse of the Starving Class* Shepard's career entered a new phase in which his plays have become more widely accessible. Referring to the "family trilogy," Richard Gilman commented, "Shepard has withdrawn noticeably from the extravagant situations, the complex wild voices and general unruliness of the earlier work. His themes, so elusive before, seem clearer now, if not pellucidly so, his vision dwells more on actual society. Physical or economic circumstances play more of a part than before."[5] For Gerald Weales, *Curse of the Starving Class* and *Buried Child* "are

4. Ibid., pp. 185–86.
5. Introduction to *Sam Shepard: Seven Plays* (New York: Bantam Books, 1981), p. xxiii.

much closer to traditional American realism than anything Shepard has ever written," though he quite correctly qualifies his statement by noting that "it is a realism that is regularly invaded by Shepard caricature . . ., by symbols . . ., by Shepard monologues . . ., by visual images which are as powerful as the verbal ones Shepard created in the early plays."[6]

Out of this blending of the concrete and the abstract, Shepard has indeed fashioned a more generally accessible theater. By no means, however, should the more recent plays be regarded as necessarily superior to the earlier ones. Each play is the expression of an aspiration that is part of a larger fabric of meaning. Some aspirations we may judge as higher than others—Shepard's playing for higher stakes—and, therefore, demanding of more complex expressions, but this does not privilege them aesthetically. It is far more valuable to examine each Shepard play as part of an ongoing enterprise—as "notes . . . on an event that's happening somewhere inside"—that has had varied manifestations over a twenty-year period: some simple, some complex; some long, some short; some working off mythic figures, some creating realistic characters; but all contributing to a larger artistic whole.

At the beginning of his career, Shepard's literary aspiration was limited by youth and lack of experience as a writer. Common to first works, he drew on his immediate situation and recreated his energetic role-playing in *Cowboys* and his recently established independence from his family in *The Rock Garden*. In retrospect, however, he did more than that. *The Rock Garden* succeeded in presenting a situation common to the American family, and it did so in striking language that was to be developed more fully in *Chicago* and *Icarus's Mother* the following year. These plays not only affirmed the promise of *The Rock Garden*, but also demonstrated that Shepard was capable of more complex theatrical renderings and that he could work on a broader cultural and philosophical plane. In the character of Stu, Shepard made it clear that the alienation of the boy in *The*

6. "Transformations of Sam Shepard," p. 43.

Rock Garden was not just the function of his place in a family but a continuing condition that was necessary to the creative personality. *Icarus's Mother* portrays this condition in almost apocalyptic images.

4–H Club replaces the rich metaphorical language of *Chicago* and *Icarus's Mother* with a leaner, more rapidly paced dialogue that is more dependent on physical action, almost in the style of vaudeville or burlesque. The characters are given something akin to routines that, through their repetitive performance, call attention to the structure of the play and the style of the acting. This structural and stylistic emphasis is more complexly and more formally treated in *Fourteen Hundred Thousand*, in which, toward the end of the play, that emphasis is combined with extended metaphorical description.

In *Red Cross* Shepard moves more firmly back to the method of *Chicago* and *Icarus's Mother*, deemphasizing structural characteristics in favor of lengthy monologues and a consideration of the nature of theatrical performance. The play's protagonist, Jim, bears much in common with Stu in *Chicago*, and the use of a bed as a central prop parallels the bathtub of the earlier play. *Red Cross* differs from *Chicago*, however, in the ironic distance from which it views the main character and the crucial role given to the maid in establishing this distance. The result is the most complex use of character in Shepard's work to this point. *La Turista*, appearing almost a year later, takes off from the characters, situations, and themes of *Red Cross* and, suitable to its greater length, develops them through a more complicated dramatic structure, a more elaborate scenic design, and a richer field of reference and association.

Melodrama Play occupies an important place in Shepard's career as his first play to use rock music. Like other Shepard plays of the period, it acknowledges its own theatricality by means of devices that distance the audience and comment on the action. It is also the first play to emphasize the problematic role of the artist in a society that treats art like a consumer product, and as such it looks forward to some of the later plays, especially *The Tooth of Crime* and *Geography of a Horse Dreamer*.

162

The complexities of *Melodrama Play* contrast with the simplicity of *Cowboys #2*. Initially appearing only a few months apart, they illustrate that dual tendency in Shepard toward ritual and spectacle on the one hand and language on the other. *Melodrama Play* has a precisely defined set, live music, extensive movement, and a relatively large cast, while *Cowboys #2* opts for a bare stage and is articulated primarily by language and numerous changes in voice by the two principal actors. Whatever its relation to the original *Cowboys*, *Cowboys #2* stands as a model for Shepard's beliefs about language and his interest in the mythic figure of the cowboy.

Forensic and the Navigators marks the beginning of a period in Shepard's work that deals with the political environment of the late sixties and early seventies. Along with *Operation Sidewinder*, *Shaved Splits*, *The Unseen Hand*, and the screenplay for *Zabriskie Point*, it clearly demonstrates a skepticism toward political solutions and a personal rather than a social perspective.

During this same period, Shepard wrote *The Holy Ghostly*, as archetypical in its themes as the others from this period are socially specific. Although its aspirations are higher than those of *The Rock Garden*, it is precisely in Shepard's first extant play that the roots of *The Holy Ghostly* are to be found. Concentrating on a father/son relationship and on those ties that both separate and bind, it is a major example of one of Shepard's most consistent concerns.

After the political plays of 1969–1970, Shepard turned inward toward more personal themes. *The Mad Dog Blues*, *Cowboy Mouth*, and *Back Bog Beast Bait* all express a sense of confusion and a need to escape from confinement. Their characters are motivated by contradictory desires and are engaged in desperate battles with fears and temptations to achieve a sense of wholeness and personal integrity.

Although the struggles of individual protagonists do not lessen in the plays that follow, the issues that give rise to the struggles are presented with new clarity and force. *The Tooth of Crime*, especially, is a work of great power. Fueled by the most striking and inventive use of language in all of Shepard, it begins a period dominated by a concern with the artist in a corrupting commercial environment, a period that includes *Geography of a Horse Dreamer*, *Angel City*, and *Suicide in B♭*. During this time, Shepard also wrote *Action*, a play that, like *Fourteen Hundred Thousand*, explores relationships among the basic theatrical elements of character, action, and language.

In the family trilogy—*Curse of the Starving Class*, *Buried Child*, and *True West*—Shepard reveals a realist strain, though not without its abstract and expressive tendencies, that has brought him wider acceptance and, consequently, a greater degree of prominence. He also broadens his examination of the American family, moving far beyond the limited aspiration of *The Rock Garden*. It is these plays, along with *Fool for Love*, that have most projected the tragic vision of American life that links Shepard to Eugene O'Neill.

In a sense *Cowboys* and *The Rock Garden* are the first scenes in a play that has not yet been concluded. The characters of this play go offstage only to reenter in new costumes and at other stages in their lives. They sometimes appear in unexpected locations and are often in transit from place to place, but like old acquaintances, their actions, speech, and behavior are familiar and call to mind sharply etched images from the past. Ice's denunciation of Pop in *The Holy Ghostly* is a replaying in more virulent form of the boy's alienation from the man in *The Rock Garden*; the latent potential for murder between the brothers of *True West* echoes the more subdued conflict between Duke and Drake in *Melodrama Play* and the overt aggression of Crow toward Hoss in *The Tooth of Crime*; the inability of Eddie to commit himself to May in *Fool for Love* links him to Weston in *Curse of the Starving Class*, who is always "looking for it out there somewhere"; and throughout all the plays are the guiding metaphors of the road, the movies, suburban American culture, the pop-music industry, and the frontier West.

Although some of Shepard's plays are undoubtedly among the best works of the American theater, his significance as a playwright emerges most fully from a consideration of all his plays as a coherent body of work. Unfor-

164

tunately, many of Shepard's plays are no longer in print and are seldom if ever produced. As a result, portions of the Shepard landscape are obscured, and the attention is focused on features that are prominent but not always among the most interesting or characteristic. The need is to bring all of Shepard's plays into the light and to correct a situation in which so little is known about such an important writer.

The contradiction between his fame and public knowledge of his plays has been intensified by the mechanisms of modern publicity. His 1979 Pulitzer Prize made his literary importance "official," and his acting career has made him known to a wider public, but publicity has taken both of these and turned Shepard into a star. "After one of the previews of *The Right Stuff*," wrote Pete Hamill, "in which Shepard plays test pilot Chuck Yeager, someone turned to me and said, 'John Glenn? To hell with John Glenn. Sam Shepard for president.'" Although this enthusiastic endorsement was prompted by the portrayal of Yeager that Shepard gives in the film, it is articles like Pete Hamill's that focus public attention and help establish the notion of stardom in the public mind. At the same time, Shepard has resisted the attempt of publicity to market him by granting few interviews and consistently refusing to talk about his personal life. He has built up a wall of privacy around himself that exists both on and off camera. Talking to him between takes of a new film, *Country*, Hamill perceived a privacy that is "more a strategy for a writer who works hard than some slickly calculated device to build up a personal mystique." Watching him on the set behind the wheel of a truck, Hamill describes Shepard as "glancing off at the horizon, as if wishing he could put the truck in gear, tell everyone to leave him alone, and drive off into the blackness."[7]

Whether Shepard will resist the temptations of stardom and actually "drive off into the blackness" remains to be seen. His 1981 confession of shame in "being an actor in a movie at all and provoking . . . stupid illusions" must still

7. "The New American Hero," pp. 75–78.

hang over his head.[8] At the same time, his film work has been of high caliber, and he has chosen his roles carefully, all the while maintaining a literary output that would be the envy of most other writers: since 1977 he has written five major plays, three shorter theater pieces, two books of prose and poems, and a screenplay for one of Europe's most important film directors. Nevertheless, the balance he strikes between the theater and the cinema—he has also indicated a desire to write and direct his own film[9]— will play a major part in determining the direction of his career.

Whatever Shepard's ultimate relation to film, he is at heart a writer. In his essay "Language, Visualization, and the Inner Library," he made clear exactly what that means: "It seems that the more you write, the harder it gets, because you're not so easily fooled by yourself anymore. . . . Even so, writing becomes more and more interesting as you go along, and it starts to open up some of its secrets. One thing I'm sure of, though. That I'll never get to the bottom of it."[10] Destinations? Sam Shepard is still on the road.

8. *Motel Chronicles*, p. 41.
9. *New York Times*, 29 January 1984, section 2, p. 26.
10. "Language, Visualization, and the Inner Library," p. 219.

SAM SHEPARD CHRONOLOGY

1943   Born 5 November at Fort Sheridan, Illinois. Father: Samuel
        Shepard Rogers; mother: Jane Schook Rogers.

1943–1955   Family moves from army base to army base, includ-
             ing a stay on Guam.

1955   Family settles in California, eventually residing in Duarte.

1962   Shepard joins Bishop's Company Repertory Players and
        tours the United States.

1963   Shepard arrives in New York and moves into the East Vil-
        lage.

1964   First plays produced: *Cowboys* and *The Rock Garden* (Theatre
        Genesis, New York, 10 October).

1965   *Up to Thursday* (Theatre 65, New York, 10 February).
        Dog and *Rocking Chair* (La Mama Experimental Theatre
        Club, New York, 10 February).
        Chicago (Theatre Genesis, 16 April).
        Icarus's Mother (Cafe Cino, New York, 16 November).
        4–H Club (Theatre 65).

1966   *Fourteen Hundred Thousand* (Firehouse Theatre, Minne-
        apolis).
        Red Cross (Judson Poets' Theatre, New York, 28 April).

1967   *La Turista* (American Place Theatre, New York, 4 March).
        Melodrama Play (La Mama Experimental Theatre Club, 18
        May; winner Obie Award, distinguished play).
        Cowboys £2 (Old Reliable, New York, 12 August; Mark
        Taper Forum, Los Angeles, November).
        Forsenic and the Navigators (Theatre Genesis, 29 December;
        Astor Place Theatre, New York, 1 April 1970; winner Obie
        Award, distinguished play).
        Excerpt from *The Rock Garden* included in the revue *Oh!
        Calcutta!*
        Received Rockefeller Foundation grant.

1968 Co-author, screenplay for *Me and My Brother*, directed by Robert Frank.
Received Guggenheim Foundation grant.

1969 *The Holy Ghostly* (La Mama New Troupe, on tour).
The Unseen Hand (La Mama Experimental Theatre Club, 26 December; Astor Place Theatre, 1 April 1970).
Marries O-Lan Johnson.

1970 *Operation Sidewinder* (Vivian Beaumont Theatre, Lincoln Center, New York, 12 March).
Shaved Splits (La Mama Experimental Theatre Club, 20 July).
Co-author, with Michelangelo Antonioni and others, *Zabriskie Point*, directed by Michelangelo Antonioni.
Appeared in film *Brand X*, directed by Win Chamberlin.
Son Jesse born.

1971 *The Mad Dog Blues* (Theatre Genesis, 4 March).
Cowboy Mouth, co-written with Patti Smith (Transverse Theatre, Edinburgh, 2 April; American Place Theatre, 29 April, with Shepard and Patti Smith in the cast).
Back Bog Beast Bait (American Place Theatre, 29 April, on the same program with *Cowboy Mouth*).
Screenplay for *Ringaleevio*.
Shepard, wife O-Lan, and son Jesse move to England.

1972 *The Tooth of Crime* (The Open Space, London, 7 July; winner Obie Award, distinguished play).
Blue Bitch (BBC).
Hawk Moon published (collection of stories, poems, and monologues).

1973 *Nightwalk* (contributor, along with Jean-Claude Itallie and Megan Terry).

1974 *The Geography of a Horse Dreamer* (Theatre Upstairs, London, 2 February; directed by Shepard).
Little Ocean (Hampstead Theatre Club, 25 March).
Action (Theatre Upstairs, September; American Place Theatre, 4 April 1975; Magic Theatre, San Francisco, 1975, directed by Shepard; winner Obie Award, distinguished play).
Shepard and family return to the United States and settle in California.

1975 *Killer's Head* (American Place Theatre; Magic Theatre on

168

double bill with *Action*, directed by Shepard).
Traveled with Bob Dylan's Rolling Thunder Revue for the purpose of writing a film script; film never realized.

1976   *Angel City* (Magic Theatre, 2 July; directed by Shepard).
Suicide in B♭ (Yale Repertory Theatre, New Haven).
The Sad Lament of Pecos Bill on the Eve of Killing His Wife (Bay Area Playwright's Festival, San Francisco, 22 October).
Received Brandeis University Creative Arts Medal.

1977   *Inacoma* (Magic Theatre).
Curse of the Starving Class (Royal Court Theatre, London; American premiere, Public Theater, New York, 14 February 1978; winner Obie Award, best new play, 1977).
Rolling Thunder Logbook published (account of his travels with the Rolling Thunder Revue).

1978   *Seduced* (American Place Theatre).
Buried Child (Magic Theatre; winner Obie Award, distinguished play, and Pulitzer Prize, 1979).
Tongues, co-authored with Joseph Chaikin (Magic Theatre).
Acts in film *Days of Heaven*, directed by Terence Malik.

1979   *Savage/Love*, co-authored with Joseph Chaikin (Public Theatre, on a bill with *Tongues*).

1980   *True West* (Magic Theatre, 10 July).
Receives Obie Award for "sustained achievement" of his career as playwright.
Acts in film *Resurrection*, directed by Daniel Petrie.

1981   Acts in film *Raggedy Man*, directed by Jack Fisk.

1982   *Motel Chronicles* published (collection of autobiographical prose pieces and poems).
Acts in film *Frances*, directed by Graeme Clifford.

1983   *Fool for Love* (Magic Theatre, directed by Shepard); winner four Obie Awards, including best play and best director.
Acts in film *The Right Stuff*, directed by Philip Kaufmann; nominated for Academy Award for best actor in a supporting role.

1984   Screenplay for *Paris, Texas*, directed by Wim Wenders.

INDEX